THE HOLINESS IN THE CHURCH

BY

REV. RAOUL PLUS, S.J.

TRANSLATED FROM THE ORIGINAL BY

MOTHER MARY ST. THOMAS

THE NEWMAN PRESS   Westminster, Maryland

1950

Lithographed By
WICKLAND - NALLEY INC.
Westminster, Md.

CONTENTS

PART I

SOURCES OF HOLINESS

PART II

HOLINESS IN ACTUAL PRACTICE

THE HOLINESS IN THE CHURCH

INTRODUCTION

HISTORY relates that a bishop of Warsaw asked the Pope for some relics for his Cathedral. " Stoop down, and pick up a little earth; every atom of Polish soil is a relic," was the answer.

Is there any region, however little it may be Catholic, to which these words may not be applied?

In face of the Church's claim to give saints to the world, some with a scornful smile will say: " The Church is dead! or if she lives at all it is a life without vital force. She has no longer power to produce saints."

Let us listen to some of these imperturbable prophets. They are named Proudhon, Michelet, Léon Denis, Aulard, Guignebert. . . . About the year 1860, when Renan's *Life of Jesus* appeared, Proudhon went so far as to write: " Let devout souls take their passports in advance, for in less than ten years there will no longer be left a single priest to administer the Holy Oils." *The Life of Jesus* has not been the death of vocations; Christ has still His faithful people and His ministers in spite of difficulties and persecutions, and the Gospel has in no way lessened its requirements nor lost its capacity to produce saints.

Victor Hugo had just published *Les Contemplations*. Michelet took offence at the poem: " Written at the Foot of a Crucifix." " The world, my dear sir, begs you not to forget it. I think it would ask you to sacrifice the six lines to the Crucifix. The Crucifix is the chief weapon against us; it is for us an Indian tomahawk. . . . When Christianity is no longer in the state of a vampire (neither dead nor alive), but honestly dead, peaceful and at rest, like India, Egypt and the Roman Empire, then only may we defend in it all that is defensible. Until then *no*. It is our enemy."

Ten days later, on May 15th, 1856, Michelet repeated the offence: " The dead themselves do not wish us to think too much of the dead. This I extend to the Christian past and to this great corpse: Christianity. Its present sterility is enough in itself to warn us that we must seek elsewhere."

Let us set aside the contradiction there is in presenting Christianity at the same time as dead and as terribly formidable (vampire, tomahawk). Let us only deal with the assertion as to sterility. Is it possible to be so blind as this? And what an extraordinary judgement to be passed by an historian! [1]

In the second edition of *Christianisme et Spiritisme* (1920) M. Léon Denis declares *ore rotundo*: " The Church is dying of an organic malady; her very source of life is attacked. For a long time past the

---

[1] In the dithyrambic eulogy just published in honour of Michelet under the grandiose title *L'Evangile Eternel*, one would have been glad if M. Guehenno had not omitted to recall the unpardonable deficiencies of his hero.

spirit of Jesus seems to have abandoned the Church. The fire of Pentecost no longer burns in and around her; that ardent flame is extinguished.''

M. Aulard, the historian of the Sorbonne, echoes this funeral oration, insolently remarking in *Le Rappel* of March 20th, 1923: '' Religious faith is so enfeebled in France that even the God of the deists, that God of Voltaire and of Cousin, has now scarcely any adherents left. Personally I know of none.''

So it may be for the deism of the Voltaires and Cousins; as for true Christians, they still exist, with all due respect to M. Aulard. The latter, believing himself to be speaking the truth of our contemporary France, writes to Guignebert: '' The French who live their religion are only a negligible minority in the nation.''

M. Guglielmo Ferrero, in a less bitter but scarcely more just strain, declares, without beating about the bush, in an article in *L'Illustration* of March 31st, 1928: '' Saints are becoming more and more rare. We gladly read their lives for the simple reason that we no longer find them in real life.'' And he attributes this singular disappearance of saints to the '' decline of the ascetical spirit.'' [1]

.   .   .   .

But supposing all these random assertions to be correct, how explain this abundant harvest of saints

[1] And again, in endeavouring to amend his argument, he makes matters worse : '' A sceptic may say that if there are no more saints, and if the ascetical spirit has declined, it is because there is no longer any need of it in our day. Precisely because to-day there is much more balance and order in the world, these sublime abnegations of which the saints were the models are no longer necessary. But perhaps this point of view is too simple.'' It is ! And moreover the argument begs the question.

3

of whom we are about to speak? Are they the sign of a dying faith, of a languishing spirit of abnegation, or again of a declining power of sanctification?

How much truer is Père de Foresta's remark: "People lament that there are no more saints! As for me I find them wherever I go." [1] Indeed, for anyone coming into close contact with souls, the evidence is as clear as daylight, and may quickly grow dazzling. Not only does the number of saints remain undiminished, but perhaps never at any other period have chosen souls been more perfect; never have they been urged by an intenser desire for Christianity in all its strength and fullness. Numbers, too, of every sort and condition, thirst after the purest holiness, a holiness which, even among children, can raise them to heights of fidelity, making them the most faithful among the faithful and carrying them as far as heroism.

What Origen said in times past is still true at the present time: "False witnesses unceasingly rise up against Jesus, and as long as evil dwells in the heart of man, accusations will arise against Him. As for Him, He holds His peace, to-day as formerly; He does not reply by words, He defends Himself

[1] We often give the name of saint to persons of very eminent virtue about whom the Church has not yet pronounced her decision, not to anticipate her decisions, which would be contrary to the prescriptions of Pope Urban VIII, but in an ordinary manner of speaking. There is, in fact, a canonized, authenticated holiness, glorified by an official, magisterial act, which is holiness in the formal sense of the word. There is, besides, the holiness of popular repute, upon which the Church will perhaps never pronounce, and yet it plays an important part in extending the Church by its power of edification and example. The very title of this book assumes mention being made of the varieties of holiness.

far more by the life of His true disciples, which speaks in an unmistakable language of its own.[1]

Certainly words are not useless; we cannot dispense with them; therefore we cannot sufficiently praise the effort attempted by the aid of books, dictionaries, etc., to bring "The Good News" within reach of those who seek it. But more convincing than this language of printed paper is the living language of history.

Now what does history say? We are about to point this out in all fairness. Doubtless these pages will offer but an outline; more will not be expected here. Our regret in not having been able to trace more than a broad outline will be lessened if, after having read this volume, the reader wishes for further information and decides to get into personal and close contact either with the teaching on the subject of Catholic holiness the better to study it, or with the biographies of Catholic saints in order to lay hold of the living soul by means of authentic documents or first-hand information.

The object of the present work is to show: first, what the Church in the twentieth century offers to her children as *means* of sanctification; second, what these means produce in those of her children who are willing to make use of them with intelligence and courage.

Hence we shall first of all, and quite briefly, make a *doctrinal review;* then a rapid enumeration of *persons and facts* which we may hope will suggest others.

Or to put this in other words:

Catholic holiness in its *principles.*

Catholic holiness in its *results.*

[1] *Contra Celsum*, Migne : *Patrologie Grecque*, XI, iii, 29.

PART I

SOURCES OF HOLINESS

If we would enumerate the supernatural riches which the Church, in the twentieth century as in every century, offers to each of her children to help him to become a saint, we are struck first of all by the fact that the Church offers to every Christian for this end a sublime *ideal* accompanied by a sure *rule*, a wonderfully coherent *doctrine* admirably adapted to man's needs, together with incomparably efficacious *helps*.

CHAPTER I

A SUBLIME IDEAL AND SURE RULE

Summary.—What is the Christian ideal? To become
" another Christ." What was it for our Lord to be
" Christ "? To carry out perfectly every will of the
Father for love of Him. What is it for the Christian
to be " Christ "? The same thing : to be a living
" ecce."

As possible deviations arising from personal views
are to be feared, our Lord has set a maternal but
firm authority by the side of this magnificent ideal,
namely, the authority of the Church.

" THE holiness of the Gospel speaks to my heart,"
confessed Jean Jacques Rousseau. It is very good
of the great dreamer to make us this avowal. Must
we not class ourselves among the least interesting
specimens of humanity if we do not feel ourselves
won over by the sanctifying power of the Gospel,
above all if we take pains to study and penetrate
into it, and do so according to the authentic
interpretation of the faithful Bride, the Catholic
Church?

What in fact is the ideal of our Saviour's religion?
It is: " Be ye perfect." And according to what
model? " Be ye perfect as My Heavenly Father
is perfect." He does not tell us to restrict ourselves
to reproducing the virtue of one saint or another.

9

That is but the preliminary. We must tend to nothing less than reproducing the holiness of God Himself.

And as the model might appear to be too far beyond us, the invisible Holiness made Himself visible: the Word became our example. Christ, the Incarnate Word, comes to show us in a human manner how to imitate the Divine Holiness. "He who sees Me sees My Father." By carefully contemplating the Son and reproducing His virtues we are sure of being in the right way towards attaining some resemblance with the Father.

For this reason is Christ's Figure raised towering above the world upon the tragic and imposing gibbet of Calvary—it must be seen by all. Does love for Christ and the desire to live as faithfully as possible according to His Divine teaching diminish with the lapse of time since the Crucifixion? There could be no greater error than to think this. "A thousand times more living, a thousand times more beloved since His death than during the days He passed upon earth, Jesus Christ has become to such a degree the corner-stone of humanity that to take away His name from the world would be to shake it to its foundations." From whom does this testimony come? From a sacred orator? A Father of the Church? No, from Renan.

In the twentieth century as in preceding ages and ages long past, our Lord manifests the sublime ideal to which eager souls aspire. The holier a life is, the more there will be found in it of the substance of the Gospel. What is it to become a saint if not to assimilate to our utmost the teaching of the Beatitudes? What is it but to seek to be identified as far as possible with Christ for love of

Him? Should not the vocation of every Christian be to imitate the Master? Certainly; but whilst the greater number stop half-way, the saints go on to the end. Christ loved *in finem*; they, too, wish to go unto the end in love. Some among them prefer to practise one particular virtue rather than another, or lay stress on some detail in the Gospel or some point of doctrine, as we shall see in the almost infinite diversity we are about to study. But under this diversity there is always one unvarying characteristic, namely, burning love for our Saviour Jesus, Whose likeness they long to reproduce as little imperfectly as possible.

And even now all is by no means said. The Church proposes to the Christian and requires of him not only to imitate Jesus, but to be a continuation of Him, to be His double, His living replica, to become in a word " another Christ." Indeed it was not only to save us that Christ made Himself one of us; He desired much more than that; He made each one of us part of Himself: " I am the Vine, you are the branches." The whole vine, *plenarium corpus Christi* as says Saint Augustine, does not mean the stem by itself. With the Vine, Jesus Christ, it bears branches engrafted upon the one Divine stock; that is to say all Christians as long as they remain in a state of grace. Christ possessing Divine life in all its fullness was nailed to the bloodstained wood on Calvary. By the opening of His wounds we were engrafted upon Him at Baptism, and became, with Him and in Him, participants of the life of the Father, of the Word, and of the Spirit.

Our vocation, then, is to live as one should live who is an integral part of Christ, one whom our

Lord Jesus desires to be an extension of Himself
as perfectly as possible, *usque ad perfectionem
ætatis plenitudinis Christi.*

In practice what does this mean? That the
Christian, in order to be truly such, should live as
much like "another Christ" as possible. This is
what the saint aims at. He knows that he cannot
imitate all the outward actions of the Saviour Jesus,
and moreover this is not required of him; but he
will strive to make his own that which constitutes
the Saviour's innermost being, namely His spirit of
absolute submission to all His Father's will. This
is the essential in Christ. The Saviour is none
other than that One Who in His twofold love for
His Father and for the human race found strength
to say eternally: "Father, I come, I give Myself.
Ecce venio"; and, in time, ratified this eternal *ecce
venio.* Bethlehem is the first step in the descent,
ecce infans; the Passion, *ecce homo,* behold the condemned Prisoner of the Antonia[1] and the Crucified
of Calvary. Behold in the Eucharist the hidden
Victim ceaselessly offering Himself from the Tabernacle, *ecce Agnus Dei.*

What word can better define a saint than this: a
living *ecce*; like Christ, a continual gift from a
motive of love. As soon as the Father's will or
desire was made known to Him, Christ at once
fulfilled it through love: love of the Father and
love of us. It was His "meat" to accomplish in
everything the Father's will, for love of His Father
and for our redemption. The saint strives to act
in all things as Christ would do. The problem for
the true Christian is not so much how to imitate
what Christ did, which is oftentimes impossible for

[1] The tower overlooking the temple.

us, but rather how to act as Christ would do in our place. And this is by no means a fiction; it is a reality. We are " other Christs "; we must fulfil the rôle demanded by this beautiful title.

It will be understood that this is the death of self-will. John the Forerunner said: " He must increase, and I must decrease." The saint thinks like John the Baptist. Self falls into the background. Ultimately it is no longer John the Baptist's dictum which remains, but that of Saint Paul: " It is no longer I that live. There is no longer any Paul in Paul; there is no longer anyone in Paul but Jesus Christ alone." The saint, like Christ, has made the Father's will his own, for love of Him, to such a degree that henceforward he no longer sees anything besides. As for himself, he no longer counts. Neither does what he thinks, or loves, or wills, any longer count. " What does God think? What does God love? What does God will? " That! " So be it, Lord, behold here I am." And he gives at each moment, as far as our nature permits, whatever God requires of him, exactly as Jesus did, to please Him and be conformed to Him. Hello says with luminous force: " The saint is one who no longer exists. God lives in him."

It is to be understood in what sense and with how much reality these words are true. L. Bertrand, in reference to Saint Teresa, speaks in the same way: " To attain possession of the one only reality, that is to say the one only love, we must yield ourselves up to this love, absolutely renounce that of creatures, and yet more, forsake this material and tangible world with ' its crowd of infinitesimal things which press us in on every side '; we must dare to make this leap into the unknown to exchange enjoyment that is immediate and certain, although ever incomplete and blended with suffering, for a far-off happiness which faith alone guarantees to us. Even when there is entire certainty of not being deceived, what heroism is involved in such an uprooting and reversion of ideas, what heroism in the audacity of such a negation! It is true holiness."

. . . .

It is good to have splendid ideals, and there are numberless souls, enraptured with the idea of this faithful and intimate reproduction of our Divine Saviour's life, eager to write with the glowing pen of love, nay sometimes with their blood, this poem of unparalleled difficulty yet so invincibly attractive, always so zealously begun but never achieved, which is the soul's perfect resemblance to Christ.

Yet as the danger of illusions, the exaggeration of personal feelings, the more or less chimerical imaginations which are apt to trouble the best wills in the world, are ever to be feared, and furthermore that all its rules may be powerfully and securely turned to account, our Lord has placed the authority of the Church at the side of the Gospel.

Would the complete definition of Catholic holiness be given in saying: It is the Gospel of Jesus Christ lived as nearly as possible? No; to complete the definition it is necessary to add: Under the ægis of the requisite authority of the Church.

Imitation, enthusiastic reproduction, for love of Christ crucified, according to the example and precepts He has left to us, this opens the way to the most daring generosity and the highest aspirations. Fidelity, respectful and loving submission to the Church, this without destroying anything of the enthusiasm and holy audacity, safeguards from illuminism after the style of Maglore or the naive misconceptions of a Salavin.[1]

Does the Gospel *alone* possess what is needful to make saints? Of itself, assuredly yes. But the Gospel needs to be lived and practised by human individuals having, each one, their own nature and views, their co-efficient of enthusiastic vibration, their possibility of wrong formation. To live the Gospel in detail, a living rule, a rule at once firm and supple, is needed, the human will, however good, being always subject, even and perhaps above all when it dreams of great things, to doubtful interpretations, imprudent delusions, or a too generous excess. The Gospel, as will be realized by whoever reflects a moment, invincibly calls for the Church. Jesus Christ, in order that His teaching might be maintained pure and intact, supposed a competent and infallible authority. Jesus Christ supposed the Vicar of Jesus Christ. Jesus had need of Peter. The Gospel would have served for little without an authority to apply the Gospel. The numerous sects into which Protestantism is divided is a crying proof of this.

And how does the Church act? Does she water down the Gospel? What sacrilege! Does she revise it? Certainly not that either. She applies it; and that is her rôle, her unique function it might be said, to specify as far as and whenever the case demands, the true meaning of the Gospel. To those who sin by falling short of what is ordained, the

[1] Works of Roland Dorgelès and Georges Duhamel wherein are represented would-be saints having nothing in common with authentically Catholic saints.

Church unweariedly recalls, at whatever cost to herself, the exigencies of the Gospel; rather sacrifice the conversion of a whole people, such as of Japan, than mitigate in the least degree the strict observance of the sixth commandment. To those who sin by excess, the Church recalls the necessary standard to be maintained: neither the Montanism which condemned marriage, nor the Jansenism which would have rendered Communion unapproachable, finds favour with her, and faithful to the authentic teaching of the true Gospel, she would condemn them even if she had to deprive herself of numerous members.

What would Christianity have become throughout the centuries if the Church had not been there to repress the faulty interpretations of an Arius, or a Pelagius, a Jansenius or a Lamennais; to condemn the quietism of a Mme. Guyon or the modernism of a Loisy; to refrain the restless seeking after the " marvellous " in religion, the craving for the preternatural; to blame a corrosive philosophy of dogma which at times, under a specious exterior, endangers souls? At the moment of her intervening, those whom she has in view, especially if they are lacking in Christian perception, find the Church's hand is hard. But it is not so. It is the hand of a mother, and after years have gone by, even those who were the most inclined to rebel, and, where they omit, judicious and sincere historians, have to acknowledge that the Church was right. Is not this what happens daily?

CHAPTER II

A WONDERFULLY COHERENT AND " HUMAN " DOCTRINE

Summary.—Marvellous proportion and perfect equilibrium between the different points of dogma; perfect adaptation to mankind; to the needs of the body and to the needs of the soul. Some examples : problems of love, ownership, and liberty.

WHAT is perhaps the most striking after the divinely transcendent character of the religion of the Saviour Jesus, is the perfect cohesion and clear-sighted equilibrium as regards the different points of dogma and at the same time their wise adaptation to the principles of most exact psychology.

Equilibrium in the first place. The Church maintains the benefit of trial and suffering; she unceasingly encourages joy. She professes that all men are equal; she maintains the inequality created by ownership and power. She exalts and defends liberty; she sets a rein on liberty. She wars against the excessive pretensions of reason; she approves legitimate aspirations and vindicates the sovereign rights of reason. She preaches the integrity and immutability of revelation; at the same time excels in adapting and applying it.

Meanwhile she cleaves so steadfastly to her doctrine that it is impossible to take anything away from it without overthrowing the whole edifice. At times it seems as if some detail were superfluous;

yet remove this stone and the pillar no longer stands firm. In the greater number of philosophies of life other than the Gospel, many theses are interchangeable; the exact opposite of the accepted propositions may be taken without interfering much with the system as a whole. In Catholicism all holds together, one detail is the explanation of another; the void calls for the " solid," and justly it is that which fills the place; another form would not fulfil the purpose.

Not that all doctrinal elements possess the same degree of certitude; distinction must be made between points of dogma, that which only comes near to the Faith, and that which cannot be denied without temerity, a whole hierarchy of propositions leading up from the one to the other. But we say: Each thesis in its right place and with the certainty due to it is exactly the thesis that is necessary. To say less or more in a different manner would no longer fit in; there would be a hiatus. It is only that special thesis which could possibly have agreed and which does agree.

Occasionally—and this is the starting-point of heresies and schisms—a theory arises which at first sight appears to be broader or truer than the Catholic position. " Down," they say, " with all constraint in education; encourage the right of private judgement in matters of belief; He is very austere, this crucified Galilean, we want a more accommodating leader; what is this belief in original sin? there was no flaw in human nature at the start! " Without even making appeal to the value of truth, let us await the sanction of experience and life. If a thing no longer fits in with the exigencies of our destiny, if it clashes, the truth is surely not there.

A " HUMAN " DOCTRINE

And there is not only perfect coherence between different points of doctrine, but perfect adaptation to human psychology. This is not one of the least beauties of Catholicism: although so transcendent it is the most human of all religions. " How true it is," exclaimed P. Aubry,[1] " that Christianity was made for man and man for Christianity, and both by the same Author." And to this a modern writer, referring to the Sacraments (of which we shall have to treat further on as most efficacious agents of our sanctification), adds his own testimony in saying that " they achieve that alliance between the Divine and the human which is the masterpiece of the Church and the principal cause of her success."

Let us recall, as more important here, how the plan of sanctification offered by the Catholic Church could not be better adapted or more adaptable than it is to the fundamental needs and desires of the compound human being, in that it concerns the body as well as the soul.

．　　　．　　　．　　　．　　　．　　　．　　　．

The Church, it is said, holds the body in contempt; she preaches mortification—the hair shirt, fasting and the discipline. Not certainly as an end in itself, but as a means, and one that must therefore be employed according as it is a means: to be made use of if it is of service—and who can seriously deny that it is of service to stem the tide of sensuality; to be rejected if inopportune or hurtful? The Church prefers the soul to the body, and if

[1] Professor of the Grand Séminaire at Beauvais, then missionary in China, where he died of destitution in 1882. He left several valuable works too little known. His vigorous brochure, *Le Radicalism dans le Sacrifice,* has lately been published as well as several of his other writings.

19

necessary permits or requires martyrdom; but she is opposed to duelling, to unjust war and to suicide. She takes up arms—and her arms alone are truly effectual—against that great agent of bodily decadence—debauchery, in demanding an upright life and absolute purity. She is in nowise in opposition to the harmonious development of the body, but she is on her guard against the exaggerated care of the body; the cultus of the flesh, scandalous exhibitions, brutish morals.

Yet has not Christ made every life to be a carrying of the Cross, and does not the Church glorify austerity as a pre-eminent means of sanctification?

When Christ speaks of this taking up of the Cross, He speaks of that self-denial necessary to accomplish God's will in all things and always. It is evident that the obligation differs according to the importance of the Divine will. It is very grave to transgress God's will in an important matter; to transgress it in a matter of slight importance is a venial sin. If it does not concern a precept, but a simple desire of God, the infraction is no longer named sin but imperfection. The saint aims at avoiding imperfection as far as possible. What is strictly requisite, in order not to lose grace, is fidelity in grave matters. The Church proportions the Divine requirements according to each one's measure of grace. Everything is not meant for everyone to the same extent, or rather, everything is meant for everyone, but the Church does not urge the Divine demands to the same extent for each one. Reservation being made of the minimum to be kept indefectibly, that is to say the state of grace, the field is open to every form of generosity: *omnes quidem currunt, non omnes accipiunt bravium.*

There are those who keep at the head, the main body of the company, and those at the rear.

And if the Church inculcates for everyone the practice of a certain austerity of life and for the most generous the generosities of penance, there is nothing in this that ought to astonish us. We have to live a life of grace in a fallen world; each one of us is capable of the worst. The evil beast named concupiscence may, at the most unforeseen moment, be awakened within us. " Every Christian carries on his lips the possibility of a Judas kiss." [1] Is not that more than enough to justify the virtue and practices of penance? We may add that the Church being a body, it is befitting that some should do more than their share to make up for those who do not do enough, and that others should deprive themselves in some degree of what is necessary in compensation for all those who make an abuse of what is superfluous. Moreover, the Church in her wisdom always intervenes to mitigate practices that might become too severe.[2] Neither is she unaware that austerity is so far from injuring the body that convents where the discipline is most rigorous are the very convents that bear record of the longest lives. The hair shirt kills fewer people than does dancing. And then the world, sport, fashion, do they not lay down draconian laws of their own? Why take offence when the Church speaks of mortifications, and not be alarmed at any exigency of the fashions requiring dangerously low-necked

[1] Mgr. Benson.
[2] Some excellent remarks on this point will be found in the work of L. de Grandmaison : *La Religion personelle,* ch. iv, *L'effort ascetique,* notably p. 122, text and note (Gabalda).

dresses, anti-hygienic costumes, and games in the fogs and mud in scanty attire?

The Church, while requiring the soul to exercise an energetic and constant supremacy over the body, is far from forgetting the saying which she herself suggested to Pascal: " He who would make the angel, makes the brute," and she has always energetically combated those exaggerated mystics who hold the body too cheaply as if it were something unworthy of us. Not only does she protect the human remains after death from the profanation of the crematorium, but she honours relics. The burial-ground is not, in her eyes, a rotting-vat, *puticuli*, according to the cruel pagan expression, but a cemetery, a place where one awaits, in a common dormitory, the call of the resurrection.

.   .   .   .

The programme of Catholic holiness is well adapted to the exigencies of the body, and not less so to the legitimate aspirations of the soul.

Let us take as examples three great problems: the problem of love, the problem of ownership, the problem of liberty. We mean here, by the problem of love, conjugal affection, the founding of the family. The Church offers a magnificent concept of human love, but regulates it by expecting unity and indissolubility, and this rule which at first sight appears too austere for nature, liberates it in reality, and answers to the true idea of love. He who loves, loves exclusively: unity. He who loves, loves for ever: indissolubility. A divided love is not love at all; love which keeps back part of itself is not love. There are two words which express love, and to which it must hold above all, under penalty of destroying itself. They are: " You only," and

" For ever." But for Christians, marriage does not assume the aspect of a contract only; it is a Sacrament, that is, a rite conferring Divine Grace. Human generation is not only for the continuation of human life, but also of supernatural life. When the Divine prescriptions are obeyed, then it is always a life-giving work; it intensifies the supernatural life in the individuals, and its consummation is ennobled by the symbolism of which it is the expression, seeing that the mission of marriage is to show us, who always need sensible images, the visible image of that far more beautiful but invisible union which takes place between God and the soul through the state of grace, that union with Christ of all souls living in Him.

Proudhon, a man little to be suspected of partiality for the Church's doctrine, says: " Christianity has produced the idea of true and chaste love; it regards woman not as the partner or equal of man, but as an indivisible part of himself: *os ex ossibus meis, et caro ex carne mea.* It distinguishes wedded love from other kinds of love, while the Indian confused it with fraternal love, the Arab debased it below the level of concubinage by polygamy and slavery, and the Roman compared it to paternal love by the law which apportioned to the mother a share in the inheritance equal to that of each of her children. Finally, Christianity has given to the world that most refined form of love, voluntary virginity, which, according to the Church, is naught else but the mystical union of the soul with Christ.[1]

Gonzague Truc, a non-practising Catholic, speak-

[1] Proudhon, *Système des Contradictions Economiques,* or *Philosophie de la Misère,* t. II, Guillaumin, 1846. p. 495.

ing of Christian marriage,[1] does not hesitate to write: " The Church achieved a master-stroke when she restored to family life that supernatural value of which custom and the long downfall of ancient cults had dimmed the remembrance. She has transformed the most perilous of contracts into a Divine institution, and she has strengthened with Divine aids an agreement which nature tends to dissolve as soon as it is made; she has blessed and consecrated the passing attraction of the sexes one for another, has sanctified human generation, and, in fact, made God concerned in the conservation of the race, by endowing married people and their descendants with moral virtues and securing the perpetuation of the human race. All human desire and all human will are transient, and especially where love is concerned. Society cannot guarantee the union of husband and wife by proving to them by reasoned demonstration that their remaining together is necessary to it. It is really only Catholic marriage which can, by invoking the authority of God, wrest the united couple from their ineradicable selfishness to enlist them in the search of a higher good, and which can dare to speak of a future in reference to the most fragile of bonds."

However beautiful the idea of Christian marriage may be, and however sanctifying this state for those who will undertake all its duties, i.e. strict conjugal fidelity, lawful use of marriage rights, paternal and maternal self-sacrifice, still the Church offers the ideal of perfect chastity to those who aspire to the state of virginity. There are saints in the married

---

[1] In a book on *Les Sacrements* in which there is, however, more than one questionable statement.

state, but there are many more in that of virginity. Their enumeration, which we shall have to make further on, will make this abundantly clear.

There is one point in particular upon which the Church's requirements are taxed with exaggeration by her adversaries, and that is, the celibacy of her priests. Let us turn to the author above quoted, whose opinion on marriage is so well justified, and see what he says about Holy Orders: " It is of the essence of the priesthood that the priest comes into contact with what is Divine, and by this contact elevates himself, rises above the world, regulates morals, heals souls, and administers affairs in which he has no part. He may acquit himself badly of his task, he may be unworthy, but he is none the less, by the nature of his charge, the elect among the elect, and the delegate of Heaven, the first in rank and influence and the ' salt of the earth ' as his Originator proclaimed him."

Again let us dedicate the following wise and forcible answer to any who may protest against the celibacy of the priest: " The ignorance of the majority of the laity on this subject is past comprehension. Putting aside the fact that the most elementary sense of what is fitting seems to ask of one who is to take God in his hands, that he should make the sacrifice of the joys of family ties, and that a married priest is not by any means the ideal, who does not see to how great an extent a married pastor, although apparently nearer to his flock, must lose prestige with them? Subject to the condition of other men, he runs the risk of also sharing their downfalls; put back into the common ruck, he becomes at once commonplace. The Catholic priest, on the contrary, is made conspicuous

by the fact that his social position is unique, and
inspires respect."

. . . .

In her teaching on the use of earthly possessions
how wise is the Church and how well she understands how to ally transcendency with prudence.

She in nowise condemns—in opposition to
socialistic doctrines—the possession of private
property, however large this property may be. Of
itself, there is nothing immoral in wealth. The rich
man has his duties: duties of justice, duties of
charity. What he has belongs *to* him; on the other
hand, not solely *for* him. But he has his rights,
and in the first place that of retaining and increasing
his fortune if it has been legitimately acquired. At
the same time the Church requires a man who
possesses any wealth to be greater than his riches,
to rise superior to them, not to allow his heart to
become earth-bound, but to use what he has as if
he had it not, and be detached in spirit. Not content
with requiring from all this poverty of heart, she
glorifies the state of voluntary poverty. "What
must I do, Lord, in order to be perfect? Already
I observe the law; but I aspire after something
beyond that. What dost Thou counsel me?"
"Go, leave what thou hast, come and follow Me."
And it is therefore that in the midst of a world
which regards nothing but money, and with
unbridled course pursues the good things of the
world, the Church, whilst allowing their just place
to earthly goods and in laying down for all the law
of labour of which the great human end is the
amelioration of the lot of all, declares that it is a
higher thing to despise riches and proclaims the
glories of poverty.

A "HUMAN" DOCTRINE

There remains the greatest good that man possesses: liberty. What use does the Church require a Christian to make of it if he wishes to be a saint?

She would have him never slavishly alienate that which constitutes his dignity as man: hypnotism is forbidden, and servile fear condemned. In obedience, it is not the human creature under whose authority he is placed whom he must regard, but God Himself. To obey a creature is to be a slave; he alone is great who obeys none but God, and in authority in whomsoever it may be placed, beholds God.

The Church has ever upheld the sovereign rights of free will, denouncing all determinism. She has always contended against Calvin and the Jansenists that if man is saved or damned it depends upon himself and not upon an inevitable and barbarous predestination which would make of God an executioner and man an automaton. She maintains, in opposition to the claims of naturalism and sensualism, that man is not inevitably the victim of his instincts, that in the worst of moral environments he may, if he so wills, with God's grace, which is never lacking, avoid evil and do good; that is to say, remain holy or become holy. On the other hand, being well aware that on account of the weakness left by original sin, the habit formed by personal deviations due to the misuse of liberty and occasions from without, the Christian needs a strong will in order to remain good, the Church constantly inculcates the education of the will. What are the *Spiritual Exercises* of Saint Ignatius, the *Spiritual Combat* of Scupoli, and the whole of Christian asceticism if not a code, a series of teachings and

27

practices whereby to learn how to overcome self and leave room only for God? Besides, in demanding a maximum of personal effort, the Church never forgets that, without God, man can do nothing. She contends, against every form of Pelagianism, that without grace we can do nothing in the supernatural order, nor even, in opposition to the semi-Pelagians, enter into this domain. As Saint Ignatius says with such psychological truth: "When about to act, I must do so as if all depended upon myself; after the action, I must behave as if all had depended on God alone." The absolute sovereignty of God's rights, and the sovereign right of free will in its own sphere, could not be better asserted.

To the Christian who wants to be a saint, the Church does not forbid the use of riches, but, while requiring effective detachment from all, she commends effective poverty for those who desire it. To the Christian who wants to be a saint, the Church permits the legitimate use of human love; she commends for those who believe themselves capable of it, and will to remain virgins, the renunciation of wedded joys, of the joys of fatherhood and motherhood.

To the Christian who wants to be a saint, the Church in the sphere of liberty, allows each one, under the security of the Divine laws, the use of personal autonomy; she recognizes, however, that there is something more glorious to God than the continual use of liberty, and that is the offering, by a free and final act, of this very freedom, by entering into a bond of obedience to qualified Superiors. Has not the Church been sufficiently blamed for tolerating, accepting and ratifying the Vow of Obedience? A diminishing of the personality, cry out those who claim to be defenders of human liberty.[1] In reality, a magnificent release, and the highest use that can be made of the will. If it were a question of binding oneself to do evil, or absolutely and without any reservation, yes, the vow of obedience would be immoral. But without losing independence in many respects, to bind oneself freely on certain specified points, in view of good, what more conformable to the full expansion of the human being? Besides, there can be no mistake about this : the cloister never killed the personality of any man or woman who possessed one; on the contrary, how many personalities has the cloister served to foster and develop? Saint Thomas Aquinas was a religious, and Saint Francis Xavier also; so, too, numbers of missionaries, Sisters of Charity, apostles of youth. We do not learn that their vow of obedience impaired the strength of their personality. Besides, who would have the tenacity to follow the religious life if it produced none but attenuated, insignificant beings? The truth is that, having at one stroke shaken off every shackle, the religious feels more free for the noble tasks he has assumed. Like a soldier under his officers, he is ready to hasten wherever he is sent to defend or extend God's Kingdom. He is the truly free being. It is the world—the tyrannies of the world—that makes slaves. Do not let us reverse the terms. To serve is to reign; and the one who best understands how best to serve reigns the most gloriously.

[1] Upon this subject, see the article *Vœux*, in the last number of the *Dictionnaire Apologétique de la Foi Catholique* (Beauchesne).

CHAPTER III

ASSISTANCE OF INCOMPARABLE EFFICACY

Summary.—The incomparable treasure of Christian prayer, meditation or exterior worship; help supplied at each decisive moment in life by an appropriate Sacrament.

To offer a doctrine rich in sanctifying power, a sublime ideal in accord with the perfect comprehension of the human individual, is already very much. But it would be of small avail if the Catholic Church did not give at the same time the help needful to live this life of holiness which she sets before her children. These means of help exist and prove of efficacy beyond comparison to whomsoever chooses to use them judiciously and courageously.

. . . .

Prayer in the first place: individual prayer and exterior worship.

The beautiful work on prayer by P. Léonce de Grandmaison[1] is well known. We have already had recourse to its authority.

It is the duty of man to pay worship to God; otherwise would he not be neglecting a part—the

---

[1] We have for our own part attempted to show the value of prayer. See the two slender volumes : *How to Pray Always,* and *How to Pray Well,* published by B.O. & W.

noblest part—of his task as creature? And then prayer is an inherent need for man, a spontaneous tendency of his nature, the cry of one poor and lowly who knows himself to be dependent on One most Rich, most Powerful, most Great.

Not that Catholic prayer consists only in the prayer of supplication. Supplication is but an inferior degree of prayer, as is well pointed out in the definition given in the catechisms: Prayer is a raising up of the soul towards God to adore, praise and thank Him and beg of Him every blessing. But it is often by means of the prayer of supplication that the soul attains to higher forms and may aspire to the most beautiful of all, namely disinterested prayer, the prayer of adoration and praise.

Moreover, it is not only with words that we should pray (*vocal* prayer); it is with our whole activity directed towards God by the purity and scope of the "intention" (*essential* prayer); but the most excellent prayer, wherein is found the maximum of endeavour to come into contact with God, is *mental* prayer, which would be better named prayer of the heart. Without fear of contradiction, this certain rule may be laid down: anyone who thus prays daily—seriously, of course, and during an appreciable length of time—is, if not already a saint, at least on the right road to holiness.

Side by side with individual prayer is exterior and public worship. A humorist has said: "A man is composed of body and soul, especially of a body." No, especially of a soul; therefore our Lord insisted that true adoration is to adore in spirit and in truth. But also of a body, and that is why Protestantism is a psychological error. We need to see and touch, to feel and to represent truths to ourselves; the

Church is too good a teacher not to offer to the Christian, as instrumental to perfection, exterior ceremonies, a common and public worship, a liturgy. Undoubtedly the essential is the soul, the dispositions of the soul; but the soul wants to be helped and to be allowed to express itself by means of outward manifestations.

Many, especially at the present day, find in the exterior ceremonies of the Church a wonderful support in their ascensions towards God, and numbers of Anglicans are striving to win back those things which the iconoclasts in the time of Huss and Wycliffe, so wantonly threw overboard as useless. Are not the recent discussions on the subject of the *Book of Common Prayer* of special significance from this point of view?

.　　.　　.　　.　　.　　.　　.

But of even more avail than these ceremonies, of which the great sanctifying value consists above all in bringing invisible realities near to us, and in symbolizing the mysteries of our Lord's life and death, are the Sacraments—rites endowed with the maximum of efficacy to make the Christian, who so wishes, a saint.

Herein is a marvel. Man is poor and weak, subject to many falls. God has provided for this: at each decisive moment of life a grace-bearing rite intervenes to place at our disposal the help needed under our new circumstances.

As soon as a little child comes into this world, the Church welcomes him and invites him to the sacrament of Baptism. Born to human life, he has now to be born to Divine life. Through Adam's sin, the devil has power over this babe, in the sense at least that the devil has succeeded in depriving him of sanctifying grace, in consequence of the fall of our first parents. The Church is about to thrust the devil out of these rights. " Go out of him, and give place to the Holy Ghost! He Who bade Peter come to Him upon the water commands thee, O cursed and damned spirit." The priest next makes the sign of the Cross over the child and says to the devil: " Do thou never dare to violate this sign of the Cross." Then comes the essential rite. To the child, whom he covers with a white cloth, he addresses these words: " Receive this white garment, and see that thou bearest it without stain before the judgement-seat of God." Without stain! Every baptized person ought to be a saint.

But the devil, although cast out on that day, surely means to return. As soon as the child shall have reached the age of discretion, that is to say the age of temptation, the enemy of the human race will try to dazzle him with the glitter of false joys, and to bring about his downfall. Then, that the baptized may be strong to resist evil suggestions from without and within, the Church offers him Confirmation, and daily bread under the form of Communion. The Very Son of God, the Incarnate Word, prolongs His life upon earth under the appearance of this little particle of bread which is the Host for the purpose of giving Himself to us as often as is necessary to enable us to continue living by the Divine life, that is to say in a state of grace.

Further, should there happen to be a serious falling away, means exist of closing hell, and regaining the Divine friendship and possession of the supernatural that had been lost: this means is confession. Considered from the psychological point of view alone, what a treasure it is! Thus, as is observed by the author of that recent work upon the sacraments to which reference has already been made, "the adversaries of the Church in their superficial disputations prefer to be blind to the fact that this practice of which they only speak with loud and holy horror, is the expression of an essential need of mankind." And again: "Confession corresponds to an inherent need of the individual. And it is a trait of genius to have utilized it as the Church has done." All those who go to confession know this well. Others have but to read Huysmans' confession in *En Route*, or the confession of the strange hero in the *Journal de Salavin* by Georges Duhamel.[1] The latter says:

"Those who see things in a true light attest that the Catholic Church alone understands the sacrament of penance in its entirety. With Protestants this sacrament, reduced to its moral effects, is restricted to a practical and pedagogic admonition: it does not rise beyond earthly limits, and from this fact it may be clearly seen how the sacramental rite as originally instituted is vitiated. The rite is administered in all its fullness by the Catholic priest, who not only admonishes but unbinds, re-opens the channel of grace, re-establishes communication with God, and finally restores the soul to the only life that can be called life. He makes the gesture of absolution; all is accomplished, eternity itself is bound, one part of life flows back into nothingness, the other is directed towards radiant possibilities."

Then, if there is question of setting up a new hearth and home, the Church, knowing that the bridal pair will have need of much Divine help to

[1] These are, moreover, the only really good pages in the book, but they are perfect.

enable them to undertake the responsibilities of wedded life, offers them the sacrament of Matrimony.

Or if, on the other hand, a young man is urged by supernatural motives to devote his life to the eternal salvation of his fellow-men, the sacrament of Holy Orders is there to invest him with the necessary powers. We have already spoken on this subject.

If a Christian is on the point of going forth from this world, there is Extreme Unction instituted to aid him in his agony, or, if it pleases God, to restore to him health of the body; in any case to give him strength of soul. Thus from the cradle to the grave, the Church is there, mother-like, ready to sanctify each passing moment, helping the Christian to live his Christian life as fully as possible, to keep himself in grace that he may the better turn his spiritual riches to account, and to increase his capacity for holiness by entire fidelity to the Divine teaching and to inspirations from on high.

If every Christian is not a saint, neither our Lord nor the Church is to be blamed. Alas, we can only accuse the weakness and cowardice inherent in our human condition.

PART II

HOLINESS IN ACTUAL PRACTICE

That the Church, in the twentieth century as at every period, possesses all that is necessary to make saints cannot be doubted by anyone willing to reflect a moment on the above considerations. These are but a few beacon lights. But if he will persevere in going further in the direction indicated, his certainty will increase.

Here is quite another question. Has the Church produced these saints whom she says she is able to produce?

CHAPTER I

" ORDINARY " HOLINESS

Summary.—There are not only canonized saints, nor
even, among the generality of fervent Christians,
souls whose greater generosity makes them stand out
in special relief; apart from this, by the average
holiness of her children, the Catholic Church
manifests the transcendency of her origin.

HOLINESS, if we may so speak, admits of two
stages: on the lower, and this is already very
beautiful, is the life lived in a continual state of
grace; on the higher, this same life but lived in a
transcendent manner, and possessing, on this
account, a value of special edification or example.

In reality every Christian ought to be a saint in
the first sense of the word; faithful to his baptism,
he ought to have it at heart to fulfil integrally the
words of our Lord: " Seek ye therefore first the
kingdom of God "—which is within: the Divine life
in the depth of the soul—the things which are added
are only the remnant, the superaddition, to be put
in the second place, and, if necessary, in the background. One thing alone essentially matters: to
live in a state of grace. That existing, the rest is
no longer of any consequence.

We must not, however, suppose that this is so
easy. Divinely " upraised " by grace we yet remain
weaklings. Our Lord, Who has restored to us the

life of the Father, the Word, and the Spirit that was
so lamentably lost by Adam's sin, has not restored
to us that exemption from evil concupiscence which
at the beginning of the world was contained in the
gift of the supernatural. Our situation is hence the
following: divinely drawn towards the Most High
by the gifts of grace wherewith we are possessed,
we are yet pitiably enticed by evil or the lesser
good, especially at certain times, and some of us
more or less than others, but all occasionally. We
live in a redeemed world, but which still bears
dangerous traces of a fallen world. It needs great
courage to resist, and this saying is often proved to
be true: "The heroic state is the state of grace."

Who can tell the number of generous, hidden
souls, living their life in the fullness of the state
of grace! Do not these multitudes of daily
Communions—to give but one instance—allow us,
without knowing the secrets of hearts, to form
some idea of the state of consciences, and to see a
manifest token of the very holy, though quite
unknown, life led by many.

Even with those who fall at times, but unweariedly
endeavour to rise again, and to practise, in their
intervals of fidelity, the most beautiful virtues, is
there not many a splendid effort to live a Christian
life in the highest measure possible to their weakness, loyal strivings after holiness, which truly render
glory to God?

When it is said that the holiness of the Catholic
Church is a note of its Divine character, it is not
only a question of the supereminent holiness of
which we shall have to speak further on, the holiness
of canonized or beatified saints, or of such as
especially stand out from the generality of the

faithful; we are now speaking of that anonymous holiness, that average holiness of the faithful. The Church must be Divine to give, as she does, to the whole body of Christians, the means of keeping in this state of high moral worth surpassing the moral worth of any other analogous community whatsoever. To put this in other words, the Church is holy, not only because she excels in fashioning individual saints, but because she likewise excels in preventing the faithful, taken as a whole, from falling away, securing to them, in spite of human weaknesses, a moral conduct such as is not to be found in the same degree elsewhere. The more the history of religions is studied, the easier it is to contrast the moral life of true Catholics and those who hold other beliefs. Averroës speaks in strong terms of how far Islamism falls short of the purity demanded by the Christian creed. We are not speaking of Paganism, where the gods themselves are immoral. Even where some elevated moral ideas exist, as in Buddhism, Confucianism, Brahmanism, how far it all is from true holiness! As for the so-called Reformation, the lives and tenets of some of those who were foremost in upholding it are disconcerting to Protestants who seek examples of sainthood among their ancestors. The very adversaries of Catholicism acknowledge the transcendent moral worth of Catholicism. The Protestant Editor of the *Expository Times*,[1] coming across the assertion published by Baron Von Hugel that "the Roman Church alone produces saints," went so far as to say: "Do we agree with that? Well, yes, we grant it. We say that to find a saint you must go to the Roman Church."

[1] July, 1922, p. 145.

Not but that there may be many shortcomings among the adherents of Catholicism, we shall come to that further on, or that there may not be true virtue among adherents of other religions. Man, every man, naturally speaking and even when he is outside the pale of the truth, is capable of moral good. Moreover, as was wisely observed some years ago by the learned Abbé de Broglie, the question is not to know whether in other religions, and notably in this respect, there are resemblances —a detail which no one contests—but whether in the midst of these resemblances, important differences are to be found, traits sufficiently transcendent to demonstrate the intervention of a supernatural cause.

On this subject there is a page full of good sense by the English convert Chesterton. The Church has never held, he says, that Christians were the only good men. " If you really want to know what we mean when we say that Christianity has a special power of virtue, I will tell you. The Church is the only thing on earth that can perpetuate a type of virtue and make it something more than a fashion." Types of goodness of purely human virtue have arisen at certain periods. What is their present power of conviction, of attraction, of example? They are types " as cold as the mountains of the moon. And so it is and so it will be with the ethics which are buzzing down Fleet Street at this moment as I speak. . . . Empires break; industrial conditions change. . . . What will remain? I will tell you. The Catholic saint will remain." [1]

If saintly souls exist outside the Catholic Church

---

[1] *The Ball and the Cross*, pp. 150-151.

—as they very well may and do exist—their holiness is due to what is Catholic mixed up with their errors, or at all events to what is preached and inculcated by Catholicism. In other words, if they approach holiness, it is never through something that separates them from Catholic life, but through something that either belongs to Catholic life or that Catholic life has made its own in accordance with the teaching of its Divine Founder. Adèle Kamm, who founded the *Coccinelles*, which was later to develop into the *Union Catholique des Malades*, belonged to the so-called Reformed Church of Lausanne, and her work is the very negation of the great Protestant principle : Each one for himself, none can merit for another, the Communion of saints is a myth. On the contrary, she asserts, as does the Catholic doctrine, that we have solidarity one with another, and that the infirm or sick may unite their sufferings with those of the Saviour and so become co-redeemers of the world with Christ.

Pusey and Ward, at the time of the Oxford Movement, were men who pushed the practice of virtue to the greatest lengths. Ward wrote to his daughter: " I cannot recall any period of my life when I was without a strong desire to please God." But these two men, like many others in the ranks of Protestantism, were not and are not virtuous by reason of something specifically Protestant. On the contrary, by reason of what is common between them and Catholics.

In the same way, it is not because of those things in which they are opposed to us that certain members of the orthodox Church sometimes attain heroic traits of holiness. Nicholas II, the last Tsar, may be reproached with great weakness in governing.

43

THE HOLINESS IN THE CHURCH

None has ever thought of blaming his private life or his virtue. And what strength of soul he showed in adversity! When he asks some who had been his courtiers to go with him into exile, almost all excuse themselves; one comes three days later and then slinks away; a certain number finally go as far as the station and then disappear. At Tsarkoie, he would have given his hand to the soldiers; they refuse to take it. We know the atrocity of those long days of mean surveillance, of persecution, and the atrocity, most cruel of all, of that massacre in the middle of the night of the whole Imperial family.[1]

Some unskilled verses, but of touching nobility, were found in a notebook belonging to the Grand Duchess Olga:

" Send us, Lord, resignation,
    In the day of darkness and tempest,
    To endure this persecution from the people,
    And the sufferings that our tormentors inflict upon us.

Grant us strength, God of Justice,
    To forgive the offences of our brethren,
    And to carry with Thy patience,
    The heavy, the blood-stained cross.
    And in the day of unrest,
    When our enemies despoil us,
    Help us, Christ, our Saviour,
    To bear shame and outrages.

Lord of the world,
    God of the universe,
    Hear our prayer,
    Give peace to our soul,
    In the terrible and sorrowful hour,
    And on the threshold of the tomb,
    Breathe upon the lips of Thy servants,
    A more than human strength,
    To pray humbly for their enemies."

---

[1] Gilliard, *Le Tragique Destin de Nicholas II*; Sokoloff, *Enquête sur l'assassinat de la Famille Impériale Russe*, pp. 21 and 32, Payot.

Such sentiments have nothing in them specifically orthodox. They are Christian, and hence they combine the resignation and spirit of charity of Catholic martyrs.

CHAPTER II

EMINENT HOLINESS

Summary.—Besides the average holiness of the members of the Church taken as a whole, there is the eminent holiness of a certain number, of a great number. First of all, in the religious life, where each Institute records examples of generosity, sometimes sublime.

BEYOND this average holiness of the mass of the truly faithful, we must signalize the eminent holiness of some—as we are about to see, of a great number.

For this is a primary characteristic of Catholic holiness at the contemporary era; the present age is extremely productive of saints, more so doubtless—as could be proved without much difficulty—than even at any other period of history.

A crowd of names at once spring to mind—names either of personages authoritatively canonized or beatified, or of personages whose perfect Christian life stands out in striking relief, who will perhaps never be raised to the altar, but have left, during their earthly passage, the example of virtues so beautiful that Christian people can never be mistaken about them, and who have a valid claim to be kept in memory for the honour of God.

EMINENT HOLINESS

Every class of society, every duty of state, **every** age bring their contingent.[1]

I. In the Religious Life

In the religious life, during the nineteenth and twentieth centuries, holiness has flourished as it were spontaneously, and that in spite of oft-times very unfavourable surroundings, and of persecution at times carried on in secret, at times with open violence.

. . . . .

Men, first of all. And to begin with a saint whom the Church has lately canonized, that young Italian *Passionist,* holy rival of Aloysius Gonzaga, Gabriel del Addolorata, who died in 1862 at the age of twenty-four; attracted to the religious life by an irresistible vocation dating from a procession in honour of Mary at Spoleta, he binds himself to honour above all the Virgin of the *Stabat*: " The Sorrows of Mary are my Paradise."

Again, what a figure of the first rank is that other Italian, Don Bosco, whose labours in the cause of education are so fruitful, founder of the *Salesian Society* and of the Institute of *Our Lady Help of Christians*. On February 20th, 1927, the decrees admitting the heroic virtues of the humble priest were read in presence of the sovereign Pontiff.[2]

---

[1] According to the spirit of this series, we shall here give scarcely any biographical details; there would be too many to supply, considering the great number of names brought forward in testimony. Each one can refer for himself to the Lives mentioned and verify at the fountainhead the holiness of the personage in question.

[2] Don Bosco has since, of course, been beatified. [Trans.]

Mgr. Baunard relates in his life of Cardinal Lavigerie, how in 1883 the founder of the *White Fathers*—himself a very holy man—wished one day, at Saint Pierre du Gros-Caillou, to present the poor priest of Turin to the faithful. The Cardinal was then leading his brilliant campaign for the liberation of slaves; the society of which he was founder had just given to heaven its two first martyrs, the Fathers Deniaud and Pascal. Mgr. Lavigerie begins to speak. It is on Don Bosco, seated facing the pulpit, on whom all eyes are turned. It is he whom all want to see and hear, and he alone. During the whole of Don Bosco's stay in Paris the roads near the house where he lodged were thronged with persons wishing to gain access to the man of God. Victor Hugo himself, then nearly eighty-three years old, wished to see " the saint."

A mysterious dream had revealed his future mission to Don Bosco.

Before receiving the subdiaconate, the Venerable Jean-Claude Colin elaborated, in his mind, the rules of his future *Society of Mary*, and beheld with the eyes of his soul his first collaborators. Marcellin Champagnat, also the founder of a teaching Institute, likewise consecrated to Our Lady, " co-disciple and emulator of the Curé d'Ars " according to the title of his biography, was at first a country curate, and created, besides some wisely organized rural works, a religious family, *the Institute of the Little Brothers of Mary*, which now numbers more than six thousand members instructing more than one hundred thousand pupils.

The Church has recently beatified Michael Garicoits, the founder of the *Fathers of Betharram*, and P. Julien Eymard (1811-1868), founder of the

Fathers and the *Handmaids of the Most Blessed Sacrament.*

Sylvain Giraud, secular priest and a very popular preacher, feels invincibly attracted towards the religious life; he dreams of the Capuchin Fathers, receives in 1856 from a young subdeacon of Aix, his diocese, a medal of Our Lady of Salette; decides in 1857 to go to make his annual retreat on the holy mountain; comes away with a great devotion to the Madonna and the pilgrimage; shortly afterwards he determines to enter among the *Missionaries of Our Lady of Salette*, founded in 1852 by Mgr. de Bruillard, and was therefore one of the first to be admitted to pronounce the three vows of religion. His works are well known, and few are better calculated to win souls to holiness: *De l'Union à Dieu dans sa Vie de Victime; De l'Esprit et de la Vie de Sacrifice dans l'Etat Religieux; De la Vie d'Union avec Marie; Jésus Christ, Prêtre et Victime;* finally *Prêtre et Hostie.* P. Giraud is wholly to be found in his books. They truly reflect the soul of a saint.

Of a quite different kind of influence, but one that carried far, were: P. Bailly, of the *Augustinians of the Assumption*, who at the age of twenty, as a lecturer of Saint Vincent de Paul, does not hesitate to carry on his shoulders, to the hovels he visits, the faggots of wood he has picked up; he was later on to be one of the first promoters of Catholic journalism on a large scale and of Pilgrimages to the Holy Land; P. Marie-Antoine, apostle of the district around Toulouse, whose witty originalities in no way hindered the great austerity of his life. The deputy Lasies said of him one day during the war: "I have had in my lifetime only two great but irresistible attachments, my mother and P. Marie-Antoine." Nothing is more to the honour of Lasies and of the illustrious *Capuchin*.

Are not Fathers Ginhac and Doyle, Auffroy and Hanrion, and that wonderful P. Lenoir, chaplain to the 4th Colonial, true saints? Of the first, one well able to judge, namely P. Ramière, said: " People meet with religious and priests of rare virtue, and they say: What a holy priest! What a holy director! What a holy man! But of P. Ginhac they say without epithet: What a saint! for he is one in the full sense of the word." The Fathers Doyle and Auffroy had for a long time asked God the signal favour of martyrdom; they were both killed during the war, Fr. Doyle in going under fire to look for a wounded English officer, P. Auffroy on a road near Rethel by a German sergeant-major who had taken him prisoner and kicked him into a ditch after having given him a blow with the butt end of his revolver. Of P. Alexis Hanrion, a religious of smiling serenity in the midst of continual helplessness, the result of broken health which prevented him from giving full scope to the richest intellectual gifts, P. Doncœur has published a delightful memoir,[1] which will do good and, as we can bear witness, has already brought forth fruits of holiness in souls.

Of that apostle of the Eucharist in the army, Père Lenoir, an eye-witness could truly write: " This poor Jesuit gained such an influence over the Colonials that one must have seen it to believe it possible. It made one understand how great waves of the Spirit passed over people in the blessed track

[1] Likewise a precious diary of Retreats (Apostolat de la Prière, Toulouse).

of some converters of bygone times. The Colonials have never pretended to be little saints. And now here are regiments, brigades, a division, which, under the impression of the supernatural and of the purity radiating from P. Lenoir, were in a body transformed within a few weeks. These marred and sometimes erring souls, often ignorant of any idea of religion, opening to its influence through the charity of a saint, gave themselves up to belated grace with the eagerness of neophytes marked out for death. These men no longer went into the trenches nor forward to the attack without having received Holy Communion."

Instinctively, under the chronicler's pen, the word "saint" has arisen. The better to reveal the astounding beauty of the apostolic soul of P. Lenoir let us select a passage from his notes of a retreat, during the course of the campaign: "Death. The battle plain, or the trenches, or a bombarded shelter, or an ambulance ward such as this. Sufferings? Probably. Consciousness? Uncertain: with the grace of my good Master I trust to be ready. . . . One thing disturbs me, would disturb me at that moment: Shall I have fulfilled all that Jesus has planned for me? Shall I have reached the point that He wills for me? Shall I have saved all the souls that He looks for from me? If it were not for this question of apostolate, death would be so sweet to me! But souls to save, the reign of Jesus Hostia to extend upon earth! . . . For Him I would live till the end of the world, in no matter what sufferings. And for His sake, too, I fear death, I am afraid of not having fulfilled my task. But here again—confidence."

P. Lenoir died whilst taking absolution and the

Sacred Host to the dying on the Vardar battlefield. " To make of the 4th Colonial a regiment of
saints," he had written, " I would give my life; I
would give it for even one." He kept his word.

Many another figure comes before us. Without
wishing to be in any way exclusive, being persuaded
that each religious family would have analogous, if
not better, claims to record, but in short to cite in
preference some names in the Institute which he best
knows, the author cannot refrain from enumerating
P. Sengler, illustrious educator and true saint, who
had vowed always to accomplish what he esteemed
the most perfect; P. de Scoraille, whose life has been
given to a wide public by P. Dudon—he left in the
memory of all those who came near him the impression of a rare greatness of soul; P. de Maumigny,
whose life was almost entirely occupied in the
spiritual formation of priests, who at the end of
their theological studies are on the eve of entering
into the ministry, an original character and of
winning virtue, whose last thanksgiving to God
before quitting this earth was for having granted him
thirty-five years of suffering; P. Cros, also a man
of marked originality—too much so, said some—but
an eminent religious and a remarkable apostle of
Mary Immaculate and of the Eucharist; P. Long-
haye, a distinguished humanist and a great man of
God, whose vivid personality and true virtue P.
Lhande has made to live again.[1]

Every religious family will have its litanies of
glorious careers. The *Cistercians* will recall P. Jean,

[1] Among Belgian Jesuits a special place ought to be
reserved to P. Petit, whose life of exceptional union with
God has been written by P. Laveille (Louvain, Museum
Lessianum).

abbot of Fontfroide (1815-1895), Dom Francis Regis, founder and first abbot of La Trappe at Staoueli, or Dom Richebé, the austere abbot of Sainte Marie of the Monts des Cats in the North; the *Marists*, the far-seeing and generous P. Limagne, Superior of the College of Montlucon, first instigator of domestic training, a superb army chaplain whose death was a heavy loss. *The Order of St. Dominic*, the Fathers Chocarne, Jandel, Clérissac, not forgetting P. Didon, a personage made a subject of some discussion, but a vigorous and outstanding figure, one who knew how to accept terrible disgrace as men of God alone know how to do; nor, struck down in full vigour, P. Vuillermet, whom a terrible heart-attack should have urged to take rest, but would none the less preach the Lenten course promised at Saint Honoré d'Eylau: " I shall die within the year, and I know it will be suddenly, but I wish to be struck down in the breach," said he, some days before setting off to Paris, where death awaited him. The town of Lille loses in him an apostle of the first order, a wise director, a preacher of great discernment and a true man of God.

We shall cite, in the course of these pages, several sons of Saint Benedict. Let us mention here Dom Guéranger and his successor Dom Delatte, as well as Dom Pitra, the very dear friend of Louis Veuillot, and of Mgr. Pie. The Church made Dom Pitra a Cardinal; his respectful love for the Vicar of Jesus Christ was such that he would never enter the presence of the Pope without having first asked absolution from his confessor. Was it not of P. Muard (1809-1854), founder of the Benedictines of Pierre-qui-vire, after having been Curé of Avallon and diocesan missionary of Sens, that Montalembert said: " I do not think I have ever met anyone who more vividly aroused in my soul the idea of a saint." Austere almost to excess, he received rare communications from God. But above all his goodness of heart—" one of the roots of renown," says Saint Francis of Sales—made his reputation. One day at Pontigny a fire breaks out; P. Muard hastens to the spot and sets to work to remove some bundles of straw. " So you want to set somewhere else on fire ? " shouts out a ruffian, thrusting him with a blow of his fist against a wall. So as not to see who had treated him thus brutally, the Father shut his eyes and always refused to have any inquiry made.

The two *Redemptorists*, Fathers Albert and Henry Payen, came of a numerous and holy family, where out of six boys four entered religion; the one was an indefatigable confessor whom everyone in his town spoke of as the saint; the other, after a career of preacher and superior, died of lupus in the face in the midst of terrible suffering and an already heavenly peace. Very edifying likewise were the lives of the Fathers Desurmont and Berthe, the latter, author of a celebrated biography of the illustrious president of Ecuador, Garcia Moreno.

Among the *Brothers of the Christian Schools*, a grand figure is that Brother Joseph, the founder of the Francs-Bourgeois. Before him, Brother Philip, Superior-General during thirty-six years, founder of evening classes for adults, humble co-operator with Montalembert and Falloux, possessing, according to the saying of a great statesman, " the stuff out of which a Cabinet Minister might have been made," and organizer of ambulances in 1870. In his biography the chapter entitled " The Saint " should be read. He will be recognized as that religious whom Horace Vernet represented standing at the foot of a wall on which hung only a Crucifix. Like St. Paul, Brother Philip knew only Jesus, and Jesus crucified. Those he governed lived according to his example, and their successors have not been unworthy of it.

.   .   .   .

Women have vied with men in holiness. Doubtless even more must be said. More spontaneously generous (the Cyrenean has to be "compelled" to do his office, while Veronica is drawn by instinct to the Master), more naturally inclined towards piety, knowing, when they know how to love after a great manner, better how to love than man, less reasoning, less egotistical, and to sum up the whole matter, more "soul" than man, according to Mgr. Dupanloup's apt saying, women, above all when a strong and vigorous Rule gives the maximum return to their effort, attain to holiness with rare ease.

The line of *Carmelites* is too well known for it to be necessary to go into detail. Teresa of the Child Jesus, Elisabeth of the Trinity, of the Carmel of Dijon; Mother Teresa of Jesus, foundress of that of Paray; Marie Aimée of Jesus, of the Carmel of the Avenue de Saxe; Xaverine de Maistre; Mother Teresa of Saint Joseph, of the Carmel of Tours of whom P. Mercier has written the life; Sister Saint Peter, of the same Carmel, who, guided by the holy man of Tours, M. Dupont, so wonderfully propagated the devotion to the Holy Face; Sister Marie-Angelique of Jesus, Carmelite of Pontoise (1893-1919). These are names belonging to the history of sanctity, and several to history without qualification.

What a number of ancient Institutes, as we have pointed out as regards Carmel, have given to our era souls of the highest virtue. Who can fail to recall among the *Poor Clares*, for example, Marie Céline of the Presentation, so interesting in the history of the devotion of reparation, and that exquisite Margaret Sinclair of Edinburgh, the Teresa of the Child Jesus of Scotland, who, young girl as she is, wears constantly next her skin a wooden cross studded with nails, and lives to such a degree of union with the Saviour that she can reply to her director when he questions her: " Our Lord He is always with me; like playing with me! "

Among the nuns of the *Visitation*, Sabine de Ségur, so wrought upon by the desire of penance and corporal mortifications: God reserved to Himself to try her in otherwise austere ways. Mgr. de Ségur, her brother, used to bring his ascetical writings to read to her in the parlour, and occasionally she gave him wise counsels. Like the holy prelate, she lost her sight; then her lungs were attacked. She died at the age of thirty-nine in indescribable joy at going to see God.

Frances Chambon, or Sister Mary Martha of Chambéry, who is plunged into ecstasy, three days in succession, at the sight of a Crucifix, and seems to have been raised up by God to revive in our times devotion to the Saviour's Wounds. Sister Benigna Consolata Ferrero, bidden by our Lord to spread abroad the devotion of confidence—such an immediately evident consequence of the devotion, rightly understood, to the Sacred Heart: " If you wish to love Me, confide in Me; if you wish to love Me more, confide in Me more; if you wish to love Me surpassingly, confide in Me surpassingly."

EMINENT HOLINESS

The Sisters of Charity yield to none for generosity in virtue. Elisabeth Seton, an Episcopalian, was converted through her need for Communion. The first Superior of the Sisters of Charity in the United States, she used to say: " I look neither before nor behind, I look above."

It was to Catherine Labouré that the Blessed Virgin granted the favour of the apparitions of the miraculous medal in the Chapel of the Rue du Bac in Paris. Sister Rosalie showed her heroism during the Commune of 1870. The Countess of Saint Martial has related in *Vers les Sommets*, and *En Haut*, her heroic efforts to follow her particular vocation. Quite lately Sister Milcent, the incomparable educator among the working-classes, went to receive the reward of her generosity and intelligent zeal. Her brother, Louis Milcent, had been one of the collaborators of Albert de Mun in organizing Catholic Workers' Guilds and agricultural Syndicates. She, valiant Sister of Charity as she was, after fifteen years spent in a school in the Rue de Caulaincourt, then five years (1897-1902) in the Rue du Bac, where she devoted herself to the re-editing of school-books, founded in 1902, in the Rue de l'Abbaye, the first Syndicate for women whereby the activities of school and " patronages " were to be succeeded by professional activities. The twenty thousand women who to-day form the Syndicates of the Rue de l'Abbaye are the beneficiaries of Sister Milcent's persevering efforts; and the place given to her in the national office of the *Pupilles de la Nation* is a recognition of the social efforts she rendered for the organization of women's work.

The numerous Institutes founded in the course of the nineteenth and twentieth centuries likewise had

THE HOLINESS IN THE CHURCH

their " nursery-gardens," their *pépinières*. Their foundresses were often saints, in every case souls of consummate virtue.

There is Madeleine Sophie Barat, canonized in 1923, to whom the Institute of the *Ladies of the Sacred Heart* owes its existence, where so thorough an education is given, radiating such a beautiful Christian spirit. Her companion, Philippine Duchesne, who had to set out to the New World, was, like her, a saint,[1] and in two recent volumes are to be found characteristic monographs of some of Mother Barat's daughters. The spirit of the foundress is well kept; the fruits of holiness remain surprisingly sweet and abundant. Other teaching Institutes likewise can offer a beautiful galaxy of names : the *Ladies of Nazareth*, to cite only them, have the Reverend Mother Victorine Hélot (1813-1900) who, as Superior-General, succeeded Elizabeth Rollat, their first Superioress and foundress together with the Duchess of Doudeauville; and Mother Marie Noel (1824-1908), two lives of humble influence and absolute fidelity : hidden lives, but how fruitful!

The Sisters of Charity of Nevers had the joy of possessing the happily privileged child of Lourdes, Bernadette, so eager to be " like the others," to " do like everyone else," who, in religion, knew nothing of the mystic illuminations of certain great contemplatives. " I do not know how to meditate," she said humbly. But it was enough to see her make the sign of the Cross in the way the Madonna had

[1] We remind the reader that we in nowise intend, whenever we employ the term, to forestall the Church's judgement. We use the expression in the generally accepted sense.

taught her, to understand the depth of her union
with God.

In Belgium, Emilie d'Oultremont, Countess of
Hoogworst, founder of the now widely spread
Institute of *Marie Réparatrice*. Obliged to accompany her husband to the theatre, she wears a hair
shirt on each occasion. God gives her, notably in
the chapel of the Château de Beauffes, ineffable
communications. Become a widow, she does not
hesitate to repeat the heroic act of Saint Chantal and
leave her young children, having, however, wisely
provided for them, in order, with the approval of
competent superiors, to follow God's call. Marie-
Anne Hervé-Bazin, Simone Denniel, Valentine Riant,
are among her daughters. They do honour to their
mother.

Among the *White Sisters of Our Lady of Africa*,
founded, like the White Fathers, by Cardinal
Lavigerie, Sister Marie Clavier and Sister Marie St.
Anselm. The latter offered herself to undergo every
suffering and humiliation " thereby to make some
amends to Jesus for the sins and lukewarmness of
consecrated souls." In 1917, she specifies : " May
each day the soul of a priest or nun unfaithful to his
or her vocation be so closely bound to mine that I
may be answerable for it." " I want as cemetery,"
she said, " the burning desert strand, or to be eaten
by a negro." She died at Rennes worn out in the
service of the wounded during the war.

Again, souls certainly saintly, for several of whom
the cause has been introduced, are these: Thérèse
Couderc, the foundress, together with P. Terme,
of the *Cenacle;* long set aside and contended
against, a marvel of humility and abnegation,
triumphing over difficulties by force of patience,

and creating a wonderfully prosperous congregation;[1] Théodelinde Dubouché, foundress of the *Adoration Réparatrice;* Madeleine Ulrich, foundress of the Institute of the *Servantes du Cœur de Jésus;* Julie-Adèle de Gérin-Ricard, foundress of the *Sœurs Victimes du Sacré-Cœur,* who, with her first companions, draws up the following act: " We devote ourselves unreservedly to all that God wills of us in His mercy and in His justice; consenting to be the victims of our sins and those of all France, in union with Jesus Christ upon the Cross "; Madeleine de Smet, whom the Curé d'Ars encouraged in her way of prayer, and foundress of the *Helpers of the Holy Souls,* so fruitful and generous in deeds and virtues;[2] Jeanne Jugan, who founded the *Little Sisters of the Poor.* It was Maxime du Camp who, astounded at seeing women, several of whom were of illustrious birth, devoting their lives to the care of poor wastrels, asked the Superioress for an explanation; she led the way to the chapel, and showing the unbeliever the tabernacle in the distance: " He Who gives us courage is over there." Words recalling those of a *Brother of the Christian Schools* who, in 1871, was nursing those stricken with small-pox: " What you are doing there, I would not do it for ten thousand francs! " " But I would not do it for a hundred thousand francs," replies the Brother. " I do it for Jesus Christ."

[1] A very good biographical notice of a religious of the *Cenacle,* Antoinette Tarut (1873-1904), has been published under the title *La petite Hostie* by a religious of the same Congregation.

[2] A delightful brochure by P. Doncœur, *Vineæ florentes.* Sœur Marie-Ignace (Art Catholique, 1926).

Again among others and in great number, Saint
Marie Postel, canonized at the same time as Mother
Barat; the Venerable Marie of Saint Euphrasie
Pellitier, foundress of the *Good Shepherd of
Angers;* Blessed Jeanne Antide Thouret, foundress
of the *Sisters of Charity of Besancon;* Mother
Marie Eugénie of Jesus, first Superior-General
of the *Nuns of the Assumption,* whose life work
was connected with that of two eminent and holy
priests, Abbé Combalot—who ought to be better
known—P. d'Alzon; Mother Marie Poussepin,
foundress of the *Dominican Sisters of Charity;*
Jeanne Elisabeth Bichier des Ages, foundress of
the Institute of the *Daughters of the Cross,* who
died in 1882 and whose cause was introduced in
1891; Victoire Thérèse Chupin, whom the Marquis
Costa de Beauregard called "the sublime rag-
picker," and whom popular renown simply called
"Bonne Mère," [1] at the age of twenty-two accepting from the Chief Commissioner of Police the care
of the fallen women of Saint Lazaire, then, having
adopted the Rule of Saint Dominic, founding at
Châtillon-sous-Baigneux (Seine) the congregation
of *Our Lady of Grace* devoted to refuge work;
those two young religious of the *Little Sisters of
the Assumption,* the Pernettes as they are sometimes
named after their holy Founder, P. Pernet; Mgr.

---

[1] *Bonne Mère,* by R. P. Mortier, O.P. Sands & Co.
5s. net. In a brochure of 1868 Alexandre Dumas *fils*
wished to plead the cause of the Refugees. The final
apostrophe is interesting to one who wishes to compare
the saints and the common run of folk : " As to thee,
O man, O my fellow-man, thou whom I know in myself
and by myself, grotesque animal, detestable and sublime
creature, capable of all, even of good, as it is thou art
cause of this evil, do as I do; try to make reparation."

Landrieux and Mgr. de Liobet have written their lives quite lately.

Where are we to stop? There is no room for more. For nothing beyond a simple enumeration the pages of this brochure would not suffice. May those who are forgotten forgive us; it is always so dangerous to enumerate; it is to risk drawing down upon oneself the wrath of those who are not mentioned. In this exceptional case, as those omitted are saints, the author has nothing to fear. He is absolved in advance.

CHAPTER III

EMINENT HOLINESS—*continued*

Summary.—Devotedness of those who set out for distant lands, undaunted by toil and weariness, the cold of the Rocky Mountains, the heat of the tropics, leprosy, the ceaseless difficulties of the apostolate, the peril of death.

II. In the Missionary Life

IN a discourse given at Malines in 1862 Mgr. Dupanloup said: " Philosophers and critics, grant me the favour, for the sake of suffering humanity, to announce the following in the columns of your daily papers: ' Wanted, five hundred thousand heroes and heroines to teach dirty children their prayers and the alphabet, on condition that the said heroes and heroines continue chaste, patient and persevering, working ten hours a day for thirty sous, and receiving calumnies to supplement their salary, while refusing even permissible pleasures.' Put that in your papers: I will pay for the advertisement. . . . You laugh? You may well do so . . . and you are wrong. For this sublime army exists. One Master alone could have called it into being and inspired it: He raises and recruits it. He has armed and commanded it for eighteen centuries; and it asks no other reward than

His smile and blessing. This Master is Jesus Christ."

Mgr. Dupanloup made no distinction between those labouring in the Metropolis and those labouring in far-off lands. If to devote oneself to suffering humanity in one's own country already calls for more than ordinary generosity, how much more is wanted to leave one's country and upon an ungrateful soil, in torrid or arctic climes, grappling with difficult languages and often brutal ways and manners, endeavour to bring peoples and tribes out of darkness to Christ.

Some of the missionaries die on the way out, as for example Father Athanase Vanhove, *Assumptionist*. In 1919, when crossing the Straits of Messina, his ship, the *Chaouia*, touches a mine, explodes and founders in the middle of the night, bearing with it three *Oblate Sisters* and five *Brothers of the Christian Schools*, of whom two are drowned; the Father, refusing all human aid for himself, stays with the last of the unfortunate creatures upon deck and perishes, the victim of his bravery. In January, 1820, a bishop, Mgr. Jalabert, nine *Fathers of the Holy Spirit*, seven *Brothers of the Christian Schools* and one *Sister of Saint Joseph of Cluny*, in all eighteen, are on the way to Brazzaville *en route* for Dakar. One tempestuous night their ship, the *Afrique*, is wrecked and they are all swallowed up by the waves of the sea.

Will those who set out ever return? No, for the most part. But what of that, since such gladness is theirs![1]

---

[1] The thrilling pages on the departure of missionaries should be read in *Çà et Là* by L. Veuillot; Bk. xii, *de la Noblesse*, under the title : *Les Nobles Chevaliers de Dieu.*

An *Auxiliatrice* nun is suddenly bidden to set out for China, one of the group originally assigned having failed at the last moment. She does not hesitate an instant. This is her letter from Marseilles, March 31st, 1926, written on the eve of departure. The courageous woman will forgive us for quoting it here. These living examples of holiness seem to us striking beyond any description of holiness set forth in pious books.

" MY REVEREND FATHER,—The Divine Master has given me the great grace of calling me to the mission field. Before leaving France I write to recommend myself to your prayers. My missionary vocation is one more proof that God's greatest graces are linked with some act of fidelity that may appear very small. . . . The thought that every-thing in connection with this sudden departure comes direct from God is a great consolation to me. The sacrifice to be made is another; it is such a beautiful opportunity of proving to God that love of Him triumphs over everything else. Besides, ' to leave all is to leave so little when it is to find God Himself! ' "

The special object of certain missions is to labour among those stricken with leprosy. A courageous Alsatian nun, Sister Leopold, who had joined the *Sisters of Saint Joseph of Cluny*[1] in 1893, died of this terrible disease at Antony on July 26th, 1925. For thirteen years she had devoted herself to the care of the lepers. In 1907 she had to be sent home: she had contracted the leprosy. At first

[1] Institute founded by the Venerable Mother Javouhey, one of the bravest of women.

she did not realize this, did not want to realize it; then she made an entire oblation of herself: " If the good God had left me my health, I could only have worked on one mission; now I can occupy myself with all." And she prayed and accepted her suffering for the salvation of the world. Little by little the malady increased till she had even to be forbidden access to the tribune, whence she had been able to assist at the Holy Sacrifice and see the Tabernacle. This was now complete reclusion. " My right eye is on strike. O Jesus, pity, leave me one of them! Let us go shares like good friends." Our Lord asked her to give up everything one thing after another. " She is a saint," P. Lena, the Assistant-General of the *Congregation of the Holy Spirit*, declared after her death: " Go and pray upon her tomb; I should not be surprised if she works miracles."

Like Sister Leopold and the illustrious Belgian missionary, Father Damien, two Jesuits, Father Beyzim, a Polish priest, and Father Dupuis, once a military chaplain of the French Expeditionary Force, died of leprosy at Madagascar. There were others too. And far from daunting such apostles, the prospect of tending lepers attracts, and supernaturally enchants them. Of such is that rector of a Spanish College, P. Félix Milan, who persistently begs to go on the missions, is sent to one of the Philippines, the Isle of Cullan, named until then the Isle of Death, which he transforms into an approach to Paradise. After eleven years of ministering to the natives of the island, whose various dialects he has meanwhile to learn, he dies in the midst of his lepers, whom he has cared for like a father.

EMINENT HOLINESS

On December 25th, 1924, Father de Orgeval embarked at Marseilles for the leper island of Taiti. Previously priest at the church dedicated to Saint George in Paris, then diocesan missionary for twenty-five years, he multiplies his efforts at the beginning of the war to get appointed as chaplain. At the age of fifty-one he dreams of the missions of Oceania, makes his profession in the *Institute of the Sacred Hearts of Jesus and Mary* (the same in which the Count d'Elbée had three years before pronounced his first vows), and he is now among the lepers of Oceania.

This ardent zeal is not only to be found in rare, isolated cases. In a novitiate of the *Franciscans of Mary*,[1] a letter is read from a bishop in China asking for four Sisters to come out to nurse the lepers. There are forty Sisters; only four are wanted. Forty hands are raised begging the privilege of being allowed to go.[2]

. . . . . .

Even when missionary life is not attended by heroic perils one has to be prepared to undergo many sufferings. Bodily sufferings first of all. The contributions sent by the *Propagation of the Faith* and the *Society of the Holy Childhood* provide enough to live on for four months at the utmost, and there are twelve months in the year!

[1] The life of the foundress, Hélène de Chappotin de Neuville, has been published by P. Hygonet, O.F.M., under the title : *Une Grande Ame, Une Grande Œuvre.* " The care of lepers," she said, " is a part of our vocation as victims."

[2] On July 24th, 1924, was opened the introduction of the cause of Sister Maria Assunta, who set out one day from Italy to go to die at Chansi, where to-day she works miracles.

Sufferings from the climate, food, clothing, lodging. transit, temperature, surroundings. Sufferings from the sense of powerlessness. " How difficult souls are to win," writes a missionary in Japan. " How hard it is to make a Christian! What numbers escape us! What a handful of Catholics we are compared with them! In Japan, 193 Catholic priests against 90,000 Shintoist priests! If Europe would at least supply us with food! But over there they seem to be unaware of our efforts! "

Then there are interior sufferings. If we are to believe Abel Bonnard's book, *En Chine*, a missionary who has thus suffered told him : " When I first came out I often shed tears during the night. But at the end of about seven years of the life I began to get used to it."

In spite of these sufferings, or perhaps rather because of them, the missions attract. When Just de Bretennières is still quite a child, he exclaims, as he leans over a hole in his parents' garden, " I hear the Chinese calling me."

H. Bordeaux has related how one of his sisters, a *Sister of Saint Vincent de Paul*, was out there for long years. She had been teaching in a village, but she, too, heard China calling her. She set out. The writer went with his brave sister as far as the end of the village. Then they had to part.

" I turned round several times until we reached the bend of the road that was to hide her from me. She was standing, motionless, at the foot of a Calvary, her hands joined together and hidden in her wide sleeves after the manner of religious. Her white cornette, cut out in light against the rising shadows of evening, appeared almost as if it shone. Already the Cross in the shelter of which she stood was but dimly discernible. That was the vision I took away with me. I was not to see her again. One evening at the end of December, 1917, when I was at the front, I learnt through the office of Foreign Affairs that she had died at Pekin."

And Bordeaux adds: " When this news reached me, I was seized with a kind of fever making me want to do better, because there is a contagious virtue in these examples where one is conscious of an absolute faith, so far removed from our uncertainties and the everlasting mixed motives of our actions."

Strange torments at times await the missionary: here the tsetse fly; there, intolerable vermin. Mgr. Clut, who did so much in evangelizing Athabaska-Mackenzie, relates that when he was at Fort Rae in 1872, each occasion on which he sat to hear confessions was a real torture, as his penitents not only rid themselves upon him of their sins, but of their abundant vermin. Mgr. Grandin, O.M.I., a Vicar-Apostolic of the same region, tells what anguish gripped his heart when he visited the missionary and found him and his companions in such terrible destitution.

In order to find food at certain seasons it was necessary to fish under the ice. P. Dechaussois in his fine book, *Aux Glaces Polaires*,[1] crowned by the French Academy, clearly shows what a torture this fishing is:

" To begin with, it is necessary to go far, for in winter the fish take refuge in the depths of the great lakes, the nearest of which is at least two days journey from here. Two of our devoted Fathers

[1] Translated into English under the title *Mid Snow and Ice*.

will be four or five months away from us seeking
shelter at night under a tent of skins. If they had
only a sufficiency of wood to make a good fire to
help them to resist this temperature of from 35 to
40 centigrade degrees of cold! But no! Then,
what labour, it might even be said what martyrdom,
it is to stand all day in such cold, on an immense
frozen lake exposed to icy winds and powdery
blinding snow; to have to break the ice to a depth
of four, five, six feet, and next day having to break
it again in the same places, for during the night
the cold soon closes up these holes again; to have
to stand for hours at a time with bare hands in icy
water, and feet in the snow, which often causes
intolerable suffering. And then the fish which is
caught at the cost of so many trials has to be
brought home. So again there are two more
Fathers with two sleds drawn by dogs continually
going and coming for the purpose. These are
certainly not pleasure trips! God be praised if the
fishing succeeds under these conditions! But sometimes it fails. And then? . . . Do you understand
the meaning of this ' then '? . . . To have nothing
to satisfy a terrible hunger! . . . Happily we have
to do with Divine Providence and we can always
have recourse to prayer. . . ."

In *Souvenirs de mes Soixante ans d'Apostolat* in
Athabaska-Mackenzie, Mgr. Grouard describes those
heroic missions in the country of the Eskimos when
at certain seasons of the year the cold falls below
fifty centigrade degrees, and where for nine months
without intermission the implacable snow covers
everything. When Louis Frederic Rouquette, the
author of *L'Epopée Blanche*, was commissioned by
the French Government to pin the ribbon of the

Legion of Honour on the purple soutane of Mgr. Grandin, Vicar-Apostolic, he read the following address, which speaks volumes: " Since first coming out to Canada in 1860 he (Mgr. Grouard) has made the name of France known and loved in Alberta and as far as the farthest northern extremities. A number of geographical names are French, thanks to him. A zealous priest, and an indefatigable missionary, navigator, geographer, explorer, builder of towns, architect, painter, composer, writer, agriculturist, he is still, at eighty-five, the most intrepid pioneer of the great North. Orphans have been gathered together in the homes he has founded. He saved Mgr. Clut's life on a memorable occasion. At the peril of his own life he has protected Indian women exposed to the brutalities of their husbands; he has tended the sick, consoled the agonizing, and moreover published books on religion in eight native languages."

A like devotedness is to be found under other skies. *L'Official* of February 27th, 1927, announced in the following terms that Mgr. Gendreau and Mgr. Le Camus had been decorated by the Legion of Honour in recognition of their work in the Colonies: " Mgr. Gendreau (Pierre-Jean), Vicar-Apostolic of Western Tonkin. A great example of disinterested devotedness towards the Annamite people during fifty-three years. Rendered the highest services to the cause of France, of which he is one of the most eminent defenders in the Far East. Mgr. Le Camus (August-Jean), bishop of Fort-de-France (Martinique). For more than fifty-three years, during which he has exercised his ministry, he has ever given proof of the greatest devotedness to the interests of Martinique. Distinguished himself on the occasion of several epidemics which devastated the colony, and again notably at the time of the eruptions of Mont Pelè, which, in 1901, destroyed the town of Saint Pierre. . . ."

Together with these illustrious names we cannot but recall that of the great "Bishop of the Cannibals," Mgr. Augouard, who died worn out by his labours in 1921 after spending forty-three years in Equatorial Africa. Neither can we omit to mention all those labourers in the tropics, Jesuits of the Congo, Father Van Hexstoven, for example, whose life has been lately published, nor those *White Fathers* of the Great Lakes, Father Lourdel and Father Augustin Achte.

These two latter were both won to the missions by what was read to them in their boyhood of the life of Théophane Venard, the martyr of Tonkin— to the latter by his mother, to the former by his teacher.

"Which of you would like to go out on the missions?" asks Mme. Achte, who is holding her eleventh child upon her knee.

"I would!" cries Augustin.

"Which of you would consent to be a martyr?" asks the professor at the Petit Seminaire.

"I would!" cries young Lourdel.

And this was more than simple childish enthusiasm. Later, when someone wanted to make him a present, the boy said: "Buy me a Crucifix, which I will always wear hanging round my neck. And see that it is very solid, and of such a kind that after I have put it on, no one will be able to drag it off again, except by cutting off my head."

Passing through the Straits of Mozambique we

come to Madagascar. If we read the life of Père Boutelant, by Père Suau, or that of Père Delpeck, for example, we shall see what self-renunciation the great island calls for, and of what courage its apostles are capable.

Let us next cross the Indian Ocean. The life of Hélêne Touvé, in religion Sister Andrée of Mary Immaculate, a missionary catechist, is instructive and inspiring. So also is the life of Mgr. Rossillon. The latter has written two stirring volumes, *Les Chevaliers de la Brousse* and *Sous les Palmiers de Coromandel*, which tell something of the evangelization of Hindustan and the marvels wrought by those great pioneers who prepare the way for Jesus Christ. To cite only one extract:

" I once well knew a missionary, one of the most valiant of men, P. Jean Marie Desaubes, now dead. As often happens in India, he had one day to take a long journey on foot. Setting out before daybreak, after having said Mass, he walked the whole morning. At midday he rested under a shady tree, and as the Indians do, put three stones together and on the top a pipkin, in which to cook a little rice. Having finished his modest repast, he continued his tramp under a temperature of 106 degrees, and walked the remainder of the day. Evening came, and when, broken down with weariness, his cassock covered with red dust, and his blood almost at boiling point with the heat and exertion, he at last regained his poor hut he had barely strength left to exclaim as he sank exhausted to the ground: 'Truly to carry on such a life as this one needs to be a saint or a fool.' "

And God blesses all these sufferings and makes them bear fruit. Indians, Chinese, natives of

Madagascar and the Congo are gradually won over by the apostolate and force of example. But how laborious it all is, and who can tell all it costs to bring a single pagan to God. We who stay at home respectfully salute our brethren in distant mission fields. If there are saints anywhere on earth, they are surely there!

CHAPTER IV

EMINENT HOLINESS—*continued*

Summary.—Some great names : Vianney, Chaumont, Chevrier, Planchat, Perreyve, d'Hulst, Abbé Huvelin . . . and higher in the hierarchy, Mgr. de Ségur, Cardinal Mercier . . . Pius X.

III. In the Sacerdotal Life

WE must not be unjust. Saints are not only to be found in mission countries; our presbyteries, in town and country, contain more than one. Barrés loved to repeat that saying of Psichari to Abbé Tournebize : " People ask us if there are still any saints, and if so where they are. They have only to turn their eyes towards our presbyteries. Saints are to be found there, and in great numbers." Psichari was not mistaken.

Father Lhande's recent investigations, of which the result is given in his *Le Christ dans la Banlieu Rouge*, speaks eloquently of the merits of these priests, hidden away in some corner in or around Paris, who, without resources, habitation, generally with nothing except their personal holiness and apostolic endurance, succeed in doing wonders.

As for Spain, Mgr. M. Gonzalez y Garcia was well justified in writing *Ce qui peut un curé aujourd-*

hui. Translated into French, the brochure loses nothing of its significance. We have but to open our eyes to learn what our priests can do. And not only in Paris. Every locality has its finished types of priestly perfection, not all on the same model, but each with its own special and personal character, which further proves the comprehensiveness of our assertion.

The district of La Bresse evokes the master figure of John Baptist Vianney, that wonderful saint whose immortal character has lately been revealed anew by Abbé Francis Trochu in his thesis for the doctorate. Auvergne recalls the good Father Serres (1827-1904), first a priest at Mauriac, a born missionary; he found an orphanage, a school for the deaf and dumb, a teaching congregation of Brothers, an Institute of Little Sisters for nursing the sick, and a refuge at Aurillac. Made a Canon against his will, he obstinately refused to allow himself to be raised to the episcopate, and died at the hospice at Salers, leaving to his heirs no other fortune beyond his instruments of penance.

The clergy of Orleans include Albert Hetsch, a Protestant doctor, who became a Catholic and entered Holy Orders. The northern region supplies Abbé Thibaut and Abbé Henri Lestienne; both were military chaplains and both died for France; already before the war the first was chaplain of the garrison at Cambrai, where he was much revered; the second (1870-1915) was the initiator of the garden cities of Lille and the originator of numerous organizations for working women.

Many more names could be cited: for example, Abbé Buathier, born in the same part of the country as the Curé d'Ars, and author of *Le Sacrifice*, a book calculated to do much good. M. Vianney had once said of him: "Take care of that child; he will do great things." Then there are Abbé Henri Chaumont (1838-1896), founder of three Salesian societies, and a great spiritual director. Abbé Debrabant, priest at Marchiennes (North), at Saint-Jacques at Douai, and later Curé at Vred. He founded the college "de la Tombe" at Kain, near Tournai, and is still more famous as founder of the flourishing congregation of the *Sainte Union*. Abbé Claude Bouvier, professor at the school of Saint Maurice Vienna, whose two books, *De l'Éducation Sacredotale*, *De l'Éducation Religieuse*, will perpetuate his apostolate; a man whose simple humility could not be persuaded to accept ecclesiastical honours. " When one is a priest that is everything," he would say. He was the brother of that heroic Father Frederic Bouvier, known by his apologetic works and his studies on the history of religions; mortally wounded at Vermandovillers, he summoned up enough strength to drag himself along to give absolution to another in the agony of death, and then expired with his arms stretched out in the form of a cross.

Living as mortified a life as that of Jean Baptiste Vianney, his poverty as absolute and piety as generous, Abbé Chevrier was at first priest at the Guillotière. His devotedness was especially noteworthy at the time of the great floods at Lyons, and, at the cost of unheard-of difficulties, and with indescribable confidence in God, he founded the work of the Prado, for children in the most God-forsaken faubourgs. Always master of himself, always recollected, he gave everyone the conviction that he was a great friend of God. The people amongst whom he lived were not mistaken about him. One woman of that quarter said: " If the good God is as good as Père Chevrier, it will be nothing to me to be judged by Him at the Last Day." And another: " Is Père Chevrier a saint? I don't know if he is a saint, but I can tell you he always shuts the door after him." That may be quite an unrecognized criterion of holiness, but perhaps not so very inapt.[1]

Abbé Planchat, who was to die at the time of the Commune, was another great friend of the people. For field of action he had the hovels of the poor. One evening he sets out to visit a dying man. He is turned away from the door. It is winter-time: he sits down on a kerb-stone opposite the house, and says his rosary under the falling snow. At midnight he is still there. Suddenly a woman rushes out of the house in great agitation. Abbé Planchat hurries to meet her. She begs him make haste to go to the sick man, who shortly afterwards gives up his purified soul to God. This was the kind of thing P. Planchat was accustomed to do. Whence came this burning zeal of his? His biographer gives the answer: " The inner life of the saints can alone explain the wonders they work." If Abbé Planchat had possessed nothing beyond an active temperament his strength could not have held out during twenty such laborious years. His soul continually renewed its vigour at the eternal source of charity—God Himself. It was in the light of that glowing furnace of love that he lived and died.

[1] Besides the life of P. Chevrier, by Villefranche, consult *La Biographie* and a volume of Letters by the Abbé Chambost. See also *Le Prêtre Selon l'Evangile* or *Le Véritable Disciples de N.S.J.C.* (Vitte), a book composed by P. Chevrier for the formation of his collaborators in the work of the Prado.

At one time Abbé Planchat went to Arras to lend his support to the work of Abbé d'Halluin—then like himself associated with the *Brothers of Saint Vincent de Paul*—another friend of the poor who left behind him a widespread reputation of rare virtue.

Another priest of Arras was the Abbé Bellanger, who in the opinion of all his confrères was a saint. His life has been written and reference can be made to it. And what diocese is there that cannot lay claim to like glories!

One day Abbé Planchat's sister, a nun at Constantinople, expressed her surprise that with all his passionate desire for the evangelization of the savages he had not become a Jesuit or a Lazarist. " So you no longer feel as you used to do when, reading the acts of the martyrs, you said : ' What happiness for them! What an incomparable grace! ' If you were a missionary you might hope for a happiness such as theirs." And the humble apostle of the faubourgs explained to what manner of martyrdom God had called him. Did he foresee that in the heart of Paris he was one day to give his blood for Jesus Christ like the martyrs of China or Corea ?

An illustrious name does not prevent the priest of Jesus Christ from stooping towards the misery of his disinherited brethren. The Abbé de Préville at Boulogne-sur-Mer, Canon Costa de Beauregard at Chambéry,[1] Mgr. de Ségur, the blind prelate so devoted to his dear Parisian apprentices, can all bear witness to this. Let us linger an instant over these two last.

Camille Costa, who was to found the Bocage

[1] His monograph written by his kinsman, Mgr. Costa de Beauregard, is entitled *Une Âme de Saint.*

Orphanage, had nine brothers and sisters. As soon as he was ordained, this was the question that he set before himself: " There are two ways in which a man may give his life," he wrote, " either in laying it down once and for all for those he wishes to save, or else in detail, day by day, in giving his strength, and time, and all that he has for those he loves. It is this last way I have chosen. . . ." Many traits in his life, Henry Bordeaux somewhere says, might have been taken from a life of Saint Francis of Sales. That is saying a great deal, but it is not too much. He reminds us, too, of another figure, Vincent de Paul. A statue of that great friend of the poor adorns Canon Costa's memorial shrine. And people come to kneel there " as at the tomb of a saint," adds his chronicler.

The life of Mgr. de Ségur is better known. The masterly pages of the Marquis de Vogué, written at the time of the great blind prelate's death, should be read. Paris had only one word to express the unanimous conviction: he who had just passed away was a saint, not in the broad sense in which that word is sometimes used, but a saint in the exact and precise sense. The Church has shown herself favourable to the introduction of his cause. A petition was addressed to Pope Pius X at the time of the Eucharistic Congress at Lourdes in 1914, signed by forty archbishops and bishops, setting forth the desire to see the glorification of the one who, " with Père D'Alzon, organized the great and beautiful association of Saint Francis of Sales as an international Catholic work for the preservation of the Faith; he who was, with Mlle. Tamisier, the initiator of the Eucharistic Congresses, and one of the heralds and most ardent apostles of frequent

Communion; he who unweariedly gave his impressive preaching and ministry as confessor to the youth of France and to whom many and many Christians owe their perseverance, many and many priests their faithful response to God's call; he who at the Congress at Nevers, in 1871, proposed the Union of those groups of workmen so dear to his heart, ever inclined towards the humble and disinherited of the earth; he who, on the very day of his first Mass, after having asked the good God for some sanctifying infirmity, bore it with unalterable patience; he who, despite this cruel blindness, composed a long series of books which have nourished, consoled and converted thousands of souls; he who appeared to his generation as a model of lofty virtue and supernatural beauty, and continues to give the benefit of his example to those who study his life. . . ."

. . . .

The apostolate of high intellectuality united to a life of very great virtue is further manifested in Abbé Perreyve, Abbé de Broglie, Mgr. d'Hulst, Abbé de Tourville, Abbé Morel, Mgr. Baunard, and in a more modest but no less effectual setting—the crypt of Saint Augustine's in Paris—the holy Abbé Huvelin, whom God was to bring into the way of Charles de Foucauld to transform the fiery officer of *chasseurs d'Afrique* into the indefatigable apostle of the Tuaregs and into a martyr.

Still nearer to our own day is Cardinal Mercier, so eminently poor and detached, so desirous for the truth, such a friend of union and charity. During his illness he only repeated " Physical suffering is so small a thing." Souls alone interested him—souls with their supernatural needs. As he lay dying, he performed that beautiful act of giving his pastoral ring to his great friend, Lord Halifax, one of the prominent members of the English High Church party, with whom he had so often conferred on the union of the Churches. It is well known what a touching letter the Cardinal of Malines wrote from the nursing-home at Brussels to his priests to stimulate them for the last time to a holy life :

" *January 18th*, 1926.

" MY VERY DEAR BRETHREN IN THE PRIESTHOOD,— During my hours of recollection, while I see all human hopes fading away, and my soul remains alone with God alone, my thoughts are drawn to you more and more closely. And I have lived with you in uninterrupted intercourse. It is the priesthood at which I look in you. Deprived of the happiness of celebrating the Holy Sacrifice of the Mass, I have been associating myself throughout the day to the Mass which the Sovereign Priest, our Lord Jesus Christ, offers at every instant, through the hands of His priests, upon all the altars of the terrestrial globe. The Mass has taken in my eyes a character of intense reality, because the sacrifice of Calvary which it commemorates has appeared to me under a tangible aspect, and it has been given me to associate myself with it more actively and more directly than at ordinary times. I have also told myself that I must make you share in this grace which the good God has granted me, by inviting you, at these hours which are perhaps the last of my life, always to celebrate the Holy Liturgy of the Mass as if you were on Calvary, and to bring to it all the fervour of faith and devotion of which you are capable."

It was on October 6th, 1845, that Renan descended the stairs of the Seminary of Saint Sulpice never again to mount them. It was on the 8th of that same month, in the same year, that Newman wrote from Littlemore to one of his most intimate friends: "To-night I am expecting Father Dominic, Passionist. He is a simple, holy man. . . . I mean to ask of him admission into the One Fold of Christ." And in the One True Fold of Christ, the great Newman was in his turn a kind of saint. Comparing another eminent convert, Soloviev—*a Russian Newman*—with the English Cardinal, Mgr. d'Herbigny says most truly: "Both, even before their conversion, loved chastity so far as to bind themselves to perpetual celibacy; both loved Jesus so far as to break with the purest friendships in order to follow Him everywhere; both loved the universal Church and their country so far as to offer themselves as victims that they might obtain the union of Church and country in the Faith."

Having begun with the lower degrees of the hierarchy, we may now ascend to the highest. We have mentioned some priests; further on, in recalling the Great War, other names will occur to complete the list. We have mentioned several prelates; what beautiful traits of holiness might not still be gleaned in lives such as those of Mgr. Pie, Mgr. Gay, Mgr. Dupont de Loges, and the Cardinals Richard, Amette and Guibert. Two Archbishops of Paris, Mgr. Affre and Mgr. Darboy, were assassinated for having attempted, at the peril of their lives, to put down the revolution in the streets by showing themselves to the rioters. The life of each has sometimes been judged severely; their death must most certainly be accounted as an act of heroism.

THE HOLINESS IN THE CHURCH

At the summit of the hierarchy stands the Pope. Will Pius X soon be canonized? Some people think so. On March 15th, 1927, the venomous paper which bears the name of *L'Impartiel Francais* reproached Rome with placing everyone on the altar: " For some time past the Church has been making saints by hundreds, with all her might. There is question of beatifying Cardinal Richard . . . and also Pope Pius X." We must first of all understand one another. We are told that the Church is dead; that she no longer produces saints. And then the next day: " The Church makes saints by hundreds." Perhaps it is meant to infer that Rome canonizes no matter who it may be. Then we reply: Look at the facts;[1] compare Pius X and Anatole

[1] Moreover, the Church is very strict as regards the official authentication of sanctity. We will briefly sketch out the procedure. The bishop of the place makes a close investigation of the person in question. If the depositions as a whole appear to justify this, the documents are sent to Rome. The Congregation of Rites nominates a postulator and an advocate. The examination of the writings is made with the greatest care. A Promoter of the faith fills the office of public minister, begins his work as censor and becomes what is called " the devil's advocate." After a series of controversial debates it is decided whether or not to open the process, called apostolic, in view of Beatification; then is made the examination of miracles, of which there must be two at least. One day an English Protestant, speaking in the presence of a prelate of the Congregation of Rites, criticized the too great facility with which the Roman Church accepts certain cures as miraculous. For all reply, the prelate sent two volumes of a process then pending to the Protestant, who was much impressed when he read them, and on returning the volumes declared that if all miracles were thus proved he would unhesitatingly retract what he had said. " Well," responded the prelate, " these miracles which appear to you so well

84

France, and tell us in which you find most virtue. For our part we prefer Pius X. Of very humble extraction, a modest country curé, Joseph Sarto, by reason of intellect and virtue, was raised to the Archbishopric of Venice, and when Leo XIII died he it was whom the Conclave appointed. He was to be the Pope of frequent communions and of the combat against modernism. It was said that even in his life he wrought miracles; he has worked some since his death. Christian people have no doubt on this point: Pope Pius X was a saint.[1]

proved, have not been admitted by the congregation." If, later, two more miracles, attributed to the intercession of the Blessed, are wrought, a fresh apostolic process is commenced, with the same procedure and the same number of sittings as for the Beatification. And, if the issue is favourable, the Pope, in a Bull addressed to the whole Catholic world, proclaims the sanctity of the Blessed, announces the canonization and fixes the feasts in connection with it.

[1] See his life by René Bazin in the Flammarion collection: *Les Grands Cœurs*.

CHAPTER V

EMINENT HOLINESS—*continued*

Summary.—Holiness among women : Elizabeth Leseur,
Marie-Lucie Vrau, Madeleine Sémer . . . Maggy . . .
Pauline Jaricot . . . ; among young men : Pierre
Poyet, Maurice Retour, Déhival, Giosué Borsi . . . ;
among children : Anne de Guigne, Jeanne Garriel,
Guy de Fontgalland . . . ; among men : Léon Harmel
. . . Ozanam . . . Jean du Plessis, Matt Talbot.

IV. In the Life of the Laity

THAT there should be saints among the clergy, and
the associations representing groups of chosen souls
in the bosom of the Church, has nothing in it
surprising. The contrary would astonish us. But
further riches await those who care to seek out
the examples of perfect Christian life and exceptional virtue to be found in the mass of the
people.

All ages are represented; all classes of society.
A list which could lay the least claim to complete-
ness would yet be interminable. We can only give
some names, taken as it were at random. All who
wish to do so can refer to the details supplied by
the monographs which appear daily and show how

much our Lord is loved, how well He is served, how, in this unbelieving, restless, perverse world, islets of holiness exist. You think the night has overtaken you. Lift up your head. Innumerable golden points pierce the darkness; up above, the stars throb in vast array.

.   .   .   .

There are saints in the married state: Marie-Lucie Vrau, Elizabeth Leseur, Mme. d'Arras, Lucie Christine, Mme. Carré de Malberg, Madeleine Sémer. "As I gaze straight forward into the truth, I already see the Light," said the last of these when dying on May 7th, 1919. This was likewise the keynote to the life of each of the others.

There are saints, and in great numbers, among young girls. "To suffer and to die, but to do something!" said Marie Paulet, "a little flower of the woodland of La Vendée." It was almost in the same words that Louise de Bettignies expressed the same thought. About to enter Carmel when the war broke out, she now devoted her life to the service of her country under conditions of which none ought to be ignorant. "I well know how this will end," she said to her most intimate helper in the work, "but I shall have rendered some service. Let us make haste and do many things before we are captured."

Thus these both reasoned, as did that young apostle of the faubourgs of Liège, Marguerite Lekeux, *Maggy*, who, at the age of twenty-three, offered herself as a victim that she might obtain the protection of her brothers at the front.

Again there is Geneviève Hennet de Goutel—at one moment wavering in her faith in consequence

of indiscriminating reading, then won over by
le Sillon—who, at the time of the Great War,
hastened to Roumania to nurse the wounded. " I
have not done enough work to come back yet. I
put my trust in God. I have no longer any other
dream than that of eternal life, and I daily look
forward to it, and know that every day brings it
nearer. Life is very short." She said again: " I
should not like to die without having done something ! " Magnificent aspirations of all these souls,
so different and yet so alike!

With a more pronounced religious note, there is
Marie de la Fruglaye, who at twenty-six years old,
while still in the world, makes, with the approval
of her director, Père Ronsin, the vow of always
doing what is most perfect. She entered later at
Les Oiseaux (Congregation of Notre Dame);
returning to the world, this was the direction she
received from Pere Renault: " Give yourself to
prayer as much as you can; but above all things
keep yourself united to the will of God, present in
you by grace." And she obeyed faithfully.

Belgian on her father's side, French on that of
her mother, Mathilde de Nédonchel visits Ars.
The holy Curé, having recognized that he had
before him a soul predestined to high sanctity, gives
her counsels dictated to him by the very Wisdom of
God. It might be said that from that day forth the
Holy Spirit endowed the soul of the young girl,
and to an almost equal degree, with the virtues of
the holy priest, especially his humility, mortification, burning zeal for souls, and immense flame of
love for God. Mathilde died at the age of twenty-
three, on the eve of her departure for Carmel.
The miracles and extraordinary gifts wherewith

God has vouchsafed to glorify His handmaid, gives ground for hope that she too, like the holy Curé d'Ars, may be raised to the altar.

Likewise in Belgium, Louise Lateau, that extraordinary *stigmatisée* of Bois d'Haine, at one moment a subject of discussion, but on the truth of whose mystical state there no longer seems room for doubt; a veritable " living Crucifix set up by God on the wayside of the nineteenth century to invite passers-by to raise their hearts towards supernatural things," in the words of her latest biographers. She lived twelve years without eating or sleeping, in spite of often toilsome days, and every Friday saw the agonies of the Passion renewed in her.

A less wonderful mystic, but with incomparable devotion to God and the poor, is Mlle. Bonnefois, of Dardilly (Rhone), who has the idea of evangelizing itinerant show-people by means of a school on wheels, spends her life in the apostolate of the fair grounds and dies in a peaceful retreat at Picpus in 1914. There is likewise Pauline Jaricot, to whom is due the work begun in Lyons, now become worldwide, of the Propagation of the Faith. The Curé d'Ars, one day interrupting himself in the course of a sermon, could say of her: " Ah! my children, I myself know a person who well understands how to accept crosses, very many crosses, and bears them lovingly. It is Mlle. Jaricot." In the will of this valiant woman of Lyons was found this avowal: " I shall regret, on leaving this world, to be no longer able to adore Jesus Christ under the Eucharistic veil where He is so forsaken, so misunderstood, to this degree that I would not hesitate to stay upon earth till the end of the world if I knew how to love Him as the saints loved Him and never offend Him."

Again, that angel of the Eucharist, Jeanne-Marie Fabre, who lived from 1891 to 1922, and whose notes are one radiant outpouring of love. "The thread that runs through them and connects them together," wrote Cardinal Mercier, "is the continuous action of Providence leading this chosen soul, from the first openings to grace until the moment when, at the age of thirty, she kneels at the foot of the altar, to offer her life to God as a holocaust, for the salvation of souls, especially for the priesthood."

Closely akin through the same spirit of generosity in the offering, Séraphine Péret; under the beautiful title *Par la Croix dans la Joie*, Paule Fleury-Dives has written the memoir and given the correspondence and journal of this victim soul of humble extraction but sublime generosity.

. . . .

That there are saints among young girls is scarcely astonishing. There are, as we shall see, saints among young men. We have but to turn over the annals of teaching institutions and colleges, biographical notices, *Livres d'Or*, for example, of Sainte-Genevieve, Saint-Clement, etc.—the choice is immense. All cannot be classified under the heading of holiness, but no other word could be found to meet the case exactly. Apart from this, and among biographies published separately, what an abundant harvest remain, as for instance in *Ames des Jeunes Normands*, the notices of Bernard and Joseph Milcent, of a family of thirteen children, nephews of the Sister of Charity who filled the distinct social rôle already mentioned; or again,

Maurice Retour, whose correspondence with his betrothed is so profoundly Christian; he died a captain, aged twenty-six, at Tahure on September 27th, 1915.[1]

What wide horizons are opened out to us in the soul of Henri Delattre by his *Méditations sur le Pater*, published by M. l'Abbé Thone, which breathe a faith and love very rare at the age of twenty.

Pierre Poyet was scarcely older when he created at Normale, by his fervour, the clearness of his convictions, and the generosity of his irresistible example, the Tala party (the party of those who go to Mass). He, too, was to die young; something of him will not die, and that is the memory of his activities, and the holiness of his life. In a discourse on one of the days when the society met at Limoges, in 1909, he exclaimed: " My dear comrades, let us manifest Christ by our deeds, by our words, and by our life. . . . But for mercy's sake don't let us forget that we shall only manifest Christ if we have Him within us." As for himself, this was his great concern: "To have a soul tormented by the haunting dread of the Divine absence. . . . To listen to God's Voice speaking within me and obey it without delay." To a friend: " Does Jesus Christ take the place that He should do within you? "

Also called to do a great work, not by an oral apostolate but by the posthumous publication of his war correspondence, is that astonishing person *Déhival*. Born of a poor Alsatian family, he gives himself up while quite young to prayer and austerity. Wounded in a cavalry regiment at the

[1] His complete biography has appeared under the title *L'Un d'Eux*, by Abbé Baron (Téqui).

beginning of the war, he exchanges into the artillery at Salonica, and from there writes letters to be compared with the most elevated writings of a Lenoir or a Foucauld. *Les Etapes de Déhival dans les Voies de l'Amour* form one of the most beautiful spiritual books possible. "The intensity of this soldier's inner life is positively outstanding," a great bishop has observed.

The intensity of the inner life, the desire after perfection, was great also in Guillaume de Montferrand. His memoir by the Abbé Rouzic deserves to be read. A pupil at Florennes, previous to the war, of that remarkable Père de Gironde, who, on setting out on August 2nd, 1914, to join the forces, took this resolution: "To be heroic to the point of preventing any expulsion of the Jesuits for the future." Guillaume de Montferrand, after having first chosen the career of officer, decides, whilst making a second retreat, in favour of the religious life, but dies, alas! before being able to carry out his project.

On the other side of the mountains, what a saintly figure is that of Giosué Borsi, whose *Colloqui*, or *Entretiens*, have been so happily translated. A great admirer of Dante, confirmed in August, 1915, at the hands of Cardinal Maffi, tertiary of St. Francis, a lieutenant of notable valour, killed as soon as he had reached the front, he thus encouraged himself to refuse nothing to God: "As long as I content myself with words, it is time lost, no one believes me. When I come to act, there will be no eloquence in the world capable of resisting the mute eloquence of my deeds. Men need example and not words, because they feel that, without example, *vana est religio*." He

said again: "The only remedy is to mount higher."
Death, to come to his rencontre, had to scale the
highest summits.

What are these but units in a legion which
numbers Blondin de Saint-Hilaire, Alexis Villié,
the two de Gaillard-Bancel, Henri de Mauduit du
Plessis, so many others, so many others. We must
further complete the list when there is a question
of the war.

.   .   .   .

Christian heroism does not wait for years.
Holiness, generally the flower of ripe age, is
becoming, more than at any other period, a
precocious flower. "There will be saints among
the children"—the saying is that of Pius X, well
acquainted with that Christian generosity which,
from the earliest years, can spring up from the
practice of frequent Communion; for it is to this
practice above all that must be attributed this
budding forth of astonishing courage and truest
piety at an age which disconcerts our rather wearied
maturity. *Our masters, the little ones!* has been
said; it is exact. The child is the father of the
man. In a very true sense they give us, in the
matter of holiness, many lessons; lesson of faithful-
ness to duty: Anne de Guigné, Elisabeth Beslier,
Jeanne Garriel; lesson of love of sacrifice: Simone
de V——, Marie-Clotilde; lesson of tender love for
the Host: Germaine Hémery; lesson of touching
confidence in God and of a wonderful spirit of
faith: Guy de Fontgalland. If you care to hear
some sayings of this delightful little person which
depict him to the life, here are some uttered during
the illness which was, at the age of eleven, to carry
him off. "When I was seven years old and made

my first Communion the Child Jesus said to me:
' My little Guy, I shall take you soon; you will die
young! ' ''—'' At Lourdes last summer at the
Grotto, the Blessed Virgin told me a secret: ' Guy,
I shall not be long before I come to look for you
to carry you away to Heaven.' ''—'' Do not cry,
Mamma; I shall die in your arms, and pass from
yours into the arms of the Blessed Virgin; she has
promised me that I shall go straight to Heaven.''
—'' When my heart hurts me too much, jumping so
high that it seems it is going to break loose, I say
to Jesus: ' Make it quiet, You Who are inside it.' ''
—'' Heaven! I cannot imagine it: for me Heaven
is Jesus! ''—'' I wanted to be a priest; but Jesus
wants to make an angel of me! ''—'' I am not afraid
of anything, not even of death, because it's the door
that leads into Heaven! ''

Here are the words of another who died at
sixteen, and whose name is not given: '' I want
to be a priest, I am going to be a priest, first of all
because the little Jesus told me so on the day of my
First Communion, and we must do everything He
tells us, and then, besides, because I mean to be like
Saint John: the Apostle who loves the most! '' Thus
he spoke at eight years old. Twenty-four months
later: '' Am I too little to make the sacrifice of my
life for a big intention? Am I too young to merit
for those I love? '' Before his last illness: '' I made
the sacrifice of my life when I was little; I know what
to expect and I am not going to take it back. Whatever happens to me is the will of God; it may be
a way of helping to save others.'' His favourite
virtue, besides generosity, was simplicity: '' I do
not understand why people want to make so much
parade with the good God; when He appeared on

earth to the saints, they fell down at His feet to
kiss them; as for me, I shall not be able to help
it, I love Him so much that when I see Him I shall
throw my arms round His neck and embrace Him."

.   .   .   .

There is saintliness among men. The life of
Léon Harmel, " le bon Père of the Val des Bois,"
has just been written. " It is the supernatural
mystical aspect of this soul which explains the
whole success of his apostolate," observes Eugène
Flornoy, and the Count de Mun, well qualified to
appreciate virtue, speaks of " the heroic holiness
of his life . . . of which it suffices to say that it
went so far as the conception of an association
founded on the desire of sacrifice and of suffering
to be asked of God as a favour." His social
conception is well known; some still contest its value;
it has a future before it: " The good of the
workman through the workman and with him,
never without him; with still more reason, never
against him." When young, he had thought of the
priesthood; his director persuaded him to remain
in the world. In September, 1870, his wife lay
dying: " My beloved, I have something to tell
you that it costs me to say. Already for three
years past I have daily offered my life to the good
God that He will not take yours." To this sacrifice,
seemingly, Léon Harmel owed the long career
which was to lie before him.

Another industrialist, M. Dutilleul. Political
men: O'Connel, Chesnelong, Lelièvre, de Mun,
Paul Lerolle, Henri Bazire. In Belgium, that
great Christian, Count Woeste. In a prayer added
to his will, he had written: " Blessed be Thou,
my God, for all the graces and benefits Thou hast

showered upon me, and if I have so ill corresponded to them, forgive me, Lord. . . . Blessed be Thou, my God, for having placed me in a position to do some good and to serve the Church, and if I have been a servant unworthy of so great a grace, forgive me, Lord! " The last words of this great fighter—he was then eighty-five—were: " I give my life for my country in the Catholic cause." Another Belgian minister, accompanied by his wife, goes, in 1915, to his daughter's Clothing at the Delivrande, near Caen. The night preceding the ceremony, Mme. de Vyvere dies in her room in the hotel. What is to be done? Delay the ceremony? No, only make one change. Instead of being called Sister Mary of Gonzaga, the Sister, at her father's request, is to take the name of Mary of the Cross.

Officers: Sonis, Paqueron, Jean du Plessis; the two second-lieutenants, Paul Henry and Auguste Lefevre; the sailor, Eugene Conort; the pontifical zouave, Arthur Cuillemin; the naval lieutenant, Dupouey, the very sight of whom preached so eloquently that it converted Ghéon,[1] or at least drew him to Christ. University men: what is more beautiful in Christian language than the prayer of the great Ampere at his wife's death-bed: " My God, I thank Thee for having created, redeemed and enlightened me with Thy Divine light in making me to be born in the bosom of the Catholic Church. I thank Thee for having called me back to Thee after my wanderings; I thank Thee for having forgiven them. I feel that Thou wouldst have me live only for Thee, that every moment may be consecrated to Thee. Wilt Thou take from me all earthly happiness? Thou art the master of it,

[1] H. Gheon, *L'Homme ne de la Guerre* (N.R.F.).

O my God! My sins have deserved this chastisement. But it may be Thou wilt listen to the voice of Thy mercy: *Multa flagella peccatoris: sperantem autem in Domino misericordia circumdabit.* I hope in Thee, O my God! but I submit myself to whatever may be Thy decree: I would have preferred death. But I do not deserve Heaven and Thou dost not will to plunge me into hell. Vouchsafe to help me so that a life passed in sorrow may merit for me a good death of which I have rendered myself unworthy. O Lord, God of mercy, vouchsafe to unite me once more in Heaven to her whom Thou hast permitted me to love upon earth."

This is the rule of life he gave himself the better to fulfil the duties of his state in the plenitude of the Catholic spirit: "Work in the spirit of prayer. Study the things of this world, that is the duty of your state, but regard them only with one eye; let the other be constantly fixed upon the light eternal. Listen to the learned, but listen to them only with one ear; let the other be ever ready to catch the gentle accents of the voice of your Heavenly Friend. Write only with one hand; with the other, hold on to God's garment, as a child holds on to his father's coat. May I ever remember what Saint Paul says, and be of those ' that use this world, as if they used it not.' May my soul, from this day forth, remain united to God and to Jesus Christ."

A critic asks: Who is it speaks thus? Is it a saint who is adding a fresh chapter to the book of the *Imitation?* What an honour for Ampère that such a question could be asked.

Has not the cause of Ozanam, the illustrious founder of the Conferences of Saint Vincent de Paul, been already introduced? When walking for the last time on the Italian shore of the Mediterranean, his priest brother sees tears falling from his eyes. " Courage, we shall soon see France! " " My dear brother, it is not that. But when I think of my sins for which Jesus Christ suffered so much, how can I help weeping? " Another time while he thus speaks with tears, a gentle voice whispers: " But are you then so great a sinner? " " Child, you do not know what the holiness of God is like."

And what outstanding figures are those of Toniolo in Italy, of Ollé-Laprune, Amédée Guiard, and Philippe Gonnard, alias Claude Lefilleul, in France. After his death at the front, his comrades said of the last of these: " He was a saint and a hero." He summed up his ideal of war in these lines:

> " . . . Smile out of duty as an apostle,
> Keep a bold front for people look to us,
> And give courage to others
> Although one has none left for oneself." [1]

Then there is Lotte, the founder of the *Bulletin des Professeurs Catholiques de l'Universite*, one of the intimate friends of that strange and sympathetic Péguy,[2] whose soul was so Catholic, but whose education at a normal school of that period and the originality of his character prevented from reaching the full practice of Catholicism.

Here we may recall the last fifteen years of the life of Huysmans (1892-1907). From the time of

---

[1] . . . *Sourire par devoir d'apôtre,*
Poitriner parce qu'on nous voit,
Et donner du courage aux autres
Alors qu'on n'en a plus pour soi.
[2] Jérôme et Jean Tharaud, *Notre cher Péguy* (Plon).

his being received into the Church he did not change his style as a writer, but what a difference in his life! He no longer wrote of any but religious subjects, lived in the shadow of the cloisters, led the life of a Benedictine in the world, cultivated prayer, and desired to die clothed in the habit of an "oblate." It was not a mere lyrical form of words, this cry of the soul, but an intense and sincere prayer: "O my dear Lord, give us the grace not thus to bargain with You, to have done with ourselves once for all, to live, in short, no matter where, provided that it be far from ourselves and near to You."

At the death of Toniolo, Professor of Law in different Italian Universities, *La Scuolo Cattolica* (November, 1918) bears him this magnificent testimony: "The soul of Toniolo was holy. We do not intend to forestall the authoritative and infallible judgement which holds up supereminent holiness to the devotion and imitation of the faithful; we are taking the word in the Christian sense which, setting a human life against the standard of the evangelical perfections and finding them in perfect accordance, expresses in one word its own judgement, admiration and veneration: he was a saint."

Amédée Guiard, whose motto was to be "Very humbly," hesitates a moment between entering the priesthood and sanctifying himself in the state of a layman. His priest brother writes to him: "I do not understand you. You tell me you want to do good. Enter then as a worker and not as an amateur into the great fabric of good, which is the Church. You tell me that you want to convert and touch souls: receive then from God the mission and power of the apostles which is called the Priesthood." Amédée replies: "The laity have also their mission. The Church needs not only priests, but also poets, writers, professors, orators, who, by their pen, word, and example, combat for her in the world, and penetrate where the priest cannot gain access."

Henri de Roure said for his part: "There are perhaps some lay vocations which, under very different forms, call for as distinct a gift as the religious vocation." A remark which must be properly understood if its exact meaning is to be safeguarded, but which expresses God's desire to have saints in every state of life.

In his beautiful volume: *L'Enseignement Catholique dans la France Contemporaine*, Mgr. Baudrillart has written under the heading of "Un Saint Universitaire," a touching sketch of Léon Lefèvre, who died in 1900 at the college at Lille. "Seeing," as he himself writes, "that I have not the virtue to be a priest, I considered that the lay apostolate is not destitute of merit, that I could, by good example, do good to some soul of good-will; that I could, by bringing up in a Christian way the children whom it might please God to send me, make of them men of duty who will contribute their small part to the amelioration of the new generation, of which France has such great need."

To his fiancée: "You know, Mademoiselle, that I am a mathematician; now every mathematician knows by his daily studies that every finite quantity is zero in presence of the Infinite. . . . I have hence been convinced, with mathematical precision, that salvation ought to come before everything, in the moral order; that all natural truth is of little importance compared with the truths of faith, and

finally, that a life which does not take Jesus Christ
for its model, as far as possible, cannot be good."
Again these words: " I aspire to the perfect love
of our Lord; I have consecrated my life to Him and
I offer Him all that I am or may be worth, so as to
make Him known and loved by those around me."

Among men of good works, the holy man of
Tours, M. Dupont, Maurice Le Gattelier, the Baron
de Livois, Adolphe Baudon, the president-general
of the Conferences of Saint Vincent de Paul after
Ozanam, Doctŏr Michaux, the originator of the
Federation Sportive des Patronages de France,
whose goodness and humility were proverbial.
Someone said of him: " I have never before met
with a faith which expressed itself so forcibly with
such little help from oratory." At his death he
left 55 " regional " unions, 2,300 societies, 30,000
active members.

. . . .

In recalling all these names we have been considering true holiness. Biographies exist; reference
can be made to them. But it must not be supposed
that, in spite of its abundance, all holiness is there
contained. The most beautiful saints are perhaps
the hidden ones. The laity are not aware of them
for the most part. Happy the priest to whom is
given to come in close contact with souls and
contemplate the marvels that grace works within
them.

Undoubtedly we must avoid canonizing before
the time, over-estimating virtues, and being too
ready or too emphatic in extolling a generosity
which seems, to those truly skilled in the matter,
not above the average. A writer who is called upon
to bring before the public the soul of a saint ought

to avoid awkwardness or heaviness, and try, if he can do so, to be an artist, avoiding the style of " those great biographical works written in rather grey tints, over-burdened with details, not simplified enough," not synthetical enough, and where the attempt is made to say everything. Even if the talent of presentation is not of the first order, the benefit for the reader is still appreciable. Some complain that *Lives* abound. There can never be too many of them. Why! to discover a memorial of Tutankhamen or of the inhabitants of Herculanium, costly researches are undertaken; shall no attempt be made, then, to bring to light some hidden virtue? The most beautiful things are those which are most quickly forgotten. Honour to those who, having discovered a vein of true holiness, have not kept the treasure for themselves alone. Every priest ought to be a biographer. Owing to lack of energy, the most beautiful Divine action in souls remains unrevealed.

Sometimes it is given to a layman to see close at hand the grandeur of some obscure sanctity. Then what ecstasy is his! Each year, on the occasion of the distribution of prizes for heroism, edifying documents are sent to the Academy. What surprises are reserved to the member to whom falls the pleasant mission of choosing the most heroic deed, of giving public homage to acts of generosity crowned by modesty, the highest of virtues. " The intention of the founders of our prizes," said the Marquis de Vogue, speaking at a meeting on November 18th, 1909, " is that we should select the prize-winner from amongst those who, by a strange interversion of words, are called the lowly; whilst they might more justly be named the great ones of this world. They are the strength, the honour, the consolation of our country. We will say even more. If we want to characterize them there is only one word that is befitting, the same in every language of Christendom: they are *saints*." He added: " I know that now . . . at the outset of the twentieth century in our country, the canonizable matter, if I may so speak, is as abundant as it could be in legendary epochs. . . ."

Now this canonizable substance almost always concerns Catholic virtue; to such an extent that the enemies of the Church, finding that good " laiques " do not come in for their share, have called the Cupola "a holy water stoop turned upside down " —*un bénitier renversé*. It is useless, we believe, to blame the Academy for this, or to defend Catholic holiness against its "rivals." Statues of great men are imposed upon us in the streets. The people are not deceived; sometimes the person represented is quite unknown to them; occasionally they recognize a man of learning or science, a great politician, nay, even a persecutor in a small way; the idea of going down on their knees does not occur to them. Civil canonizations are not like those of the Church, and while the illustrious little great men of one period will long ago have fallen into oblivion, a young nun who died at the age of twenty-six, Teresa of Lisieux, or an old country parish priest, the Curé d'Ars, will still be honoured, and that by all the world. The Church alone holds the secret of glories that are immortal.[1]

[1] Upon *Les Saints de la Libre-Pensée. Essais Infructueux de Canonization Laique*, see *Revue des Objections*, September, October, 1926. Reproduced in *La Documentation Catholique*, 11 Juin, 1927, col. 1501-1505.

Her power of sanctification is such that in no matter what land, she can produce flowers of unparalleled virtue. Neither age, nor sex, as we have said, prevents anyone from becoming a saint; nor social status. Saints are to be found in apparently most humble environments, and these are not the least numerous nor the least beautiful; for example, that Augustin Bodin, son of a socialist of Ivry, who, being turned out of doors by his father for having gone to the Catholic " patronages," goes to pass the night on the glacis of the fortifications, all the more tranquilly since on opening the *Imitation* in the light of a gas-jet his eyes fall on the words: " *Of what do you complain? You have not yet resisted unto blood.*" " It seemed as if this was meant for me. And since then I have no longer suffered." One day his companions in the workshop place on his bench a Crucifix which they have bought out of derision. Augustin picks it up, kisses it, takes a hammer and nail and hangs the Crucifix on the wall. All applaud him. He died, a young aspirant to the religious life.

On Sunday, June 7th, 1925, a workman, almost a septuagenarian, dies suddenly in a street in Dublin when about to enter the church of Saint Saviour. Under his clothes are found instruments of penance which had eaten into his flesh. Who is this mysterious dead man? A humble labourer. For forty years he has slept only on a plank, and that only for four hours. From two o'clock in the morning, he prays; as soon as the churches are opened, he hears Mass until time for work. He takes his meals kneeling. None had known his saintliness during his lifetime. He dies. Interest is aroused. Within the six months following the publication of a sketch of his life, twenty thousand copies are bought up. The name of this workman: Matt Talbot.

A good weaver goes to make his annual retreat at Notre Dame du Hautmont, near Lille, and shows the Father who was preaching the retreat his rule of life. It is this: " In the morning, and immediately on rising, at half-past five o'clock, the sign of the Cross and ' Divine Heart of Jesus.' . . . I set things in order as far as necessary for the children and myself. The children go downstairs, we pray together, then they ask a blessing and each one sets off to his work. On reaching work, I make a big sign of the Cross, and say: ' My God, all this work, for your love, for the conversion of all the workmen in this factory, and for those in authority, for those who insult me.' In the evening, supper about eight o'clock; we chat a little together, then evening prayers and the rosary. The children ask a blessing and all go off to bed. On Sundays, two Masses when possible. Confession at least every fortnight and Communion every week or oftener. In the morning, until midday, visit poor families."

Vying with this weaver, a frequenter of retreat houses in the North, there is a Belgian signal-man sanctified by means of the retreats of Fayt-les-Manage. Attacked by gastritis when twenty-five, he is advised to make a pilgrimage. He sets out, but on the way reflects that this suffering is good for him and he returns home. His library consists of Saint Alphonsus de Liguori's *Visits to the Blessed Sacrament*, which he reads nearly three hundred times and thus gains the habit of almost continuous spiritual communion. He lives a pure

life, has no enemies, does all the good he can, gives
part of his wages to his father, part to the poor,
from time to time a hundred francs to the missions.

If there are saints among workmen there are so
likewise among workwomen, small employees and
servants. What a height of virtue this quite recent
simple announcement suggests: "You are asked
to assist at the funeral of Mademoiselle Aimée
Leherpeur, formerly president of the Congregation
of Christian servants of Rennes, and for sixty-six
years in the service of the Bellevue family."
Another of these unassuming servant-maids, not
being able to afford alms, goes to the Grand Seminaire, and asks as a favour to be allowed to wash
the linen of one of the future priests of the house,
over and above her own work and out of love for
the priesthood.

Another young girl, a tulle-maker in Calais, prevented by her mother from rising in the morning
to go to Communion, slips downstairs with bare
feet, escapes by an air-hole in the cellar, goes to
receive our Lord, and her mother, on awakening,
finds her lying quietly in her bed.

Does anyone dream of recording such facts? Do
they not, however, say much for the astonishing
generosity of the Catholic soul?

As for holiness, it is not only to be found at the
office, the factory and in humble trades. In 1924
the Grand Duchess Marie Adelaide, for some time
sovereign of her country of Luxemburg, died, aged
scarcely thirty. She had vowed her virginity to
God and dreamt of Carmel, when, on June 12th,
1912, she was obliged to put on the crown. On
that occasion the President of the Council thought
he might, contrary to custom, pass over the name

of God in silence. The Grand Duchess declared that, unless this necessary addition were made, she would not be present at the assembly. Each morning she heard Mass and communicated. In spite of opposition, she insisted on the solemn enthronement of the Sacred Heart in the Grand Ducal Palace. Her position during the war was a difficult one; she was constrained to abdicate. She made no difficulty about this, and was admitted to the Carmel of Modena on September 14th, 1920. Worn out by all she had gone through, she had to leave; she asked to be accepted among the pensionnaires of the Little Sisters of the Poor and began a life of devotedness to the unfortunate. Her country claimed her to take the direction of a hospital; but her end was near. After having asked her mother's permission to die, she gave up her soul. On her tomb are these words only: " Blessed are the clean of heart, for they shall see God."

CHAPTER VI

QUALITY OF HOLINESS IN OUR DAY

Summary.—Saints, in our day, are numerous. The quality of their holiness is even greater than their numerical value. Some examples during the Great War. Martyrs for the Faith. Marvellous doctrinal standard of contemporary holiness. Conversions and vocations.

IT is practically impossible to deny the numerical value of Catholic holiness at the time in which we live. But in what does its intrinsic value consist? Must we believe Renan with his bitter perspicuity when it is a question of the Church? "There are no more real saints, there are no longer any but attenuated saints."

In Volume III of the life of Louis Veuillot by his brother Eugène (p. 472) is to be found the great journalist's energetic reply to this random assertion. Yet the best refutation remains that of facts. The Catholic holiness of our day attenuated! It is perhaps the most glaring mistake that any historian could make.

What is most likely to impress the superficial observer when he compares the *Lives* of the saints written to-day with those of other days, is the marked tendency—and a very happy one—of insisting less on the idea that holiness consists above all in ecstasies, visions and extraordinary occurrences, of discriminating between history and legend in such matters, with a wiser and better informed spirit of criticism, and in insisting rather on the essential of holiness, namely unwavering fidelity, carried as far as heroism, to God's every will. This is apt to give the impression that saints of the present day are not so far removed from ourselves. In one sense this is true, but in one sense only. Modern saints are in no way inferior to those of former times, and next in order to the immense variety that saintship takes, what most strikes us is the rare purity of the holiness of the present day. We may be already convinced of this: the quality is of even greater worth than the quantity.

Is it necessary to add other traits to those already given? What could be more valorous, for example, than this episode related by P. Lhande among his stories of the Red Ring round Paris? One evening at the end of the month of October, in the year 1896, the presence of an ecclesiastic wandering through the labyrinth of lanes and alleys, of which the quarter of Cayenne, at Saint-Ouen, then consisted, aroused great excitement all along his way. In the memory of man or of woman, no blackrobe had been seen in those parts. Heedless of the groups gathered on the doorsteps or in the courts in front of the hovels, heedless of the coarse jokes and superstitious conjurations of which he was the object, the priest went on his way. Suddenly at the corner of an alley, a startled group of young hooligans appear. At the sight of a priest, several of them, stricken with panic, take to their heels, exclaiming: " Un corbeau! " (A crow.) But one more intrepid than the rest comes to a halt after having scampered off. He fixes the enemy with a defiant glance. Then stooping down, he picks up a stone out of the rut and flings it with all his might at the intruder. The missile reaches its mark. It strikes the priest full in the face, inflicting a wound. The "crow" is doubtless about to avenge himself, for he in his turn stoops down. But while the lad runs off, he hears a voice calling him. He turns round. The priest is still standing there, and far from attempting to parry the attack he simply holds up the little stone stained with his blood. "My friend," he cries out to him, "thank you . . . this stone that you threw at me shall be the first stone of the church which I am going to build in this place. . . ." The priest kept his promise, and the little stone thrown by him into the foundations of the large and beautiful church of the Rosary was the corner-stone of the building.

At the death of the wonderful Sister Saint Marguerite, of whom Louis Arnould wrote *con amore* telling of her supernatural endeavours to set at liberty the *Soul in Prison* of Marie Heurtin, a young deaf and dumb and blind girl, the historian thus gives vent to admiration: "This unexampled true story should be made known. It deserves to be read kneeling, and is like a chapter out of the Golden Legend. People say there are no longer any miracles! And here is one! . . . An existence like that of Sister Marguerite is enough to prove that of God."

In a recent volume entitled *De Pauvres Vies*, a journalist, Jean de Vincennes, has sketched the following pretty scene from life: Two Little Sisters of the Poor go to beg in the market-place; he interrogates them. People are generous it appears; cabbages, carrots, turnips, young fruit and vegetables are readily given by the vendors: "They give so willingly." "And what about those who

do not give?" "Oh well, that goes for nothing.
. . . I think only of the others!"

"In my Carlylian paradise," writes Henri Ghéon,
"the saints never entered into my calculation: the
heroes of real life simply outstripped them; without,
however, denying that, under certain conditions,
holiness can blossom forth in this world, I relegated
it to bygone ages. Through the eyes of Giotto and
Angelico, who gave me a fleeting glimpse of Heaven,
by means of medieval art, it appeared to me as a glory
that is past, having nothing in common with our
days, a hundred times more unimaginable than that
Hellenic beauty to which a modern athlete may at
need give some conception. I accepted and
respected the Christian, but for me, a saint was a
stoic. I was a passionate admirer of all excess of
love and sacrifice, but on an earthly plane, in the
human order of things."

.   .   .   .

If there was ever a period when the highest virtues
flourished, it was surely the period of the last war:
everything was on a big scale then, and acts of
devotedness inspired by an altogether natural love
of duty—for, after all, even nature of itself is capable
of what is very good—with how much more reason
did specifically Christian acts of heroism abound and
superabound.

We have mentioned P. Lenoir dying in the cornfields
of Vardar when on his way to assist the wounded on
the battlefield of Salonica; we must further mention
that Dominican, P. Berchon, spoken of by Gaudy in
the *Agonie du Mont Renaud*, who, at the peril of his
life, went to encourage the men at the first-aid
stations and take the Eucharist to the battle-line;
the Abbé de Chabrol, struck down at the moment

when, standing on the parapet with Crucifix in hand, he was giving his blessing to the tide of onslaught bounding from the trenches; that Sister Julie, a nun of Saint Charles of Nancy, who so heroically protected the wounded of Gerbévilles and risked her life in saving the sacred ciborium from the flames; Anthelme de Gibergues, who was the worthy nephew of the bishop of Valence, and left in the pocket of his aviator's coat the following will and testament:

" If one day when flying in the blue heavens I fall to earth with broken wings and so return to God, these lines bring to my mother and father the last thoughts, wishes and supreme dreams of the son they love so much.

" When my aeroplane, being mortally wounded, can do no more, when it becomes impossible to carry on my commission, and my task on earth is ended, when I am flung down only a few yards from where the battle is raging, an infinite and long-awaited peace will take possession of me, and I shall sing with all my heart *Gloria in Excelsis Deo*. . . . Oh! those few seconds before suffering and death which the world holds in such horror that it will try to hide them from you as something atrocious, you will bless them with me; they are a favour of the Sovereign Judge. As my shuddering body nears the ground, my soul will rise more lightly to unknown heights; the separation will be triumphant. It will be the complete *Magnificat*: the prayer of adoration to the One Great and Merciful God, the prayer of thanksgiving for all that has been so liberally bestowed upon me from every side, the prayer of expiation more for what I have omitted than for what I have done; and then the suppliant cry which cannot but be heard, imploring eternal life, strength and consolation for those I am about to leave, mercy and glory for our beloved France, and the coming of God's Kingdom *Adveniat regnum tuum!* This prayer will be all linked up with you, my beloved parents, for I have learnt it from your words and example during twenty-eight years. It will be sweet and calm in spite of appearances; it will breathe forth confidence and peace."

An Under-Secretary of State with very advanced opinions, who had seen the Jesuit, Lucien Chabord, "hero and mystic," at work, could not refrain from making an enthusiastic eulogy which has been often quoted. P. de Daran, drowned when *La Providence II* was wrecked in the Mediterranean, gives his blessing and absolution until his last moment to those about to be submerged in the waves. Yves de Joannis, a clerk in minor orders, grievously wounded at Fère-Champenoise, is in hospital at Troyes; to his mother who says to him: " Dear boy, you are seriously ill, it would be well for you to have the last Sacraments," he responds: " That is a surprise! Is it really true? Am I not to suffer any more than this? How good God is! I am going to Heaven without having earned it."

André Lerolle, mortally wounded at the farm of Beauregard on October 1st, 1914, expires a month later, at the age of thirty-nine. As the father of eight children, he might have remained at the depot: he did not choose to do so. Before leaving for the front he had written in his will: " I am a Catholic, and I beg my darling children never to forget that the Catholic religion alone is true; that they will continue to love our Lord Jesus Christ, as they love Him at this moment, and will not give up the habit of frequent Communion, but, on the contrary, will communicate every day if they can do so; it is the one and only means of having peace upon earth, and of being able to resist the temptation which, sooner or later, will assail them. Now I place myself in all confidence under the protection of God and the Blessed Virgin." The following resolution occurs in his notes: " To do God's will without seeking to accomplish extraordinary things, to do what God wills in the state wherein He has placed us." And this beautiful prayer: " My God, make me love suffering, so that I may not only be resigned to it, but love it as You loved it."

We cannot omit the mention of Bourjade the Oceanian as he was called by Kérillis, one of his old comrades in the squadron. This Léon Bourjade, a religious of the Society of the Sacred Heart of Issouden, is twenty-five when the war breaks out. As an aviator, he is honourably mentioned fourteen times and numbers twenty-four authenticated victories over the enemy. In November, 1918, the Aero Club of France awards him the gold medal for his feats in defensive aviation. At the end of the war he embarks for New Guinea, where he cares for the poor negroes, to whom he consecrates his life, and dies at the age of thirty-two, having already earned his reward.

Going even further than his duty, listening only to the voice of his zeal, the Abbé Marie-Joseph Margot-Duclot, missionary of Notre-Dame-du-Laus, military chaplain, hastens to the aid of a mortally wounded officer, and falls with his face towards the enemy, at the fort of Froide-Terre. A touching episode is added to this sacrifice, consummated on June 24th, 1916, which makes of the chaplain a modern Tarcisius. " A detail which makes his death unique amongst those of all the priests fallen on the field of honour is that he was shot right through the heart by a bullet which first passed through the Sacred Species borne upon his breast, and it was the head of Christ, Who was represented on the front of the pyx, as standing between the two disciples of Emmaus, which was pierced by the fatal bullet."

The Christian family is the workshop where, by preference, God fashions His saints. Louis and Antony Collard, two young Belgians who fell under the bullets of the invader at the fortress of Liège on July 18th, 1918, had at home learnt both Christian courage and patriotic valour. Their memoir, to which Mgr. Heylen, bishop of Namur, wrote the preface, breathes devotion and purity.

As we see, not only are there priests, religious or seminarists in the ranks of saintship. There are laymen, often quite young men, but whose Christian virility exerted a wide influence. Great events can either raise up great souls, or else simply reveal them. Some souls in order to be brought to light have need of dark days, lacking which their life would perhaps have been small and insignificant. Others would have become great without the war, but the war gave them the opportunity of taking their measure. Of such was Clement Tonnerre, one of a family which gave eleven saints to the Church. He was the disciple and friend of the Count de Mun, and not satisfied with expressing all his love for the people in the beautiful pages entitled *Pourquoi Nous Sommes Sociaux*, devoted himself in his part of Picardy to multiply agricultural syndicates. On the breaking out of the war, he refused to remain at the Staff Office, and chose to join the troops. "The man who does his duty," he said, "deserves no praise; he is a cad if he holds back; he is only worthy of praise if he does more than his duty." He was killed when commanding the Zouaves, after having been eight times honourably mentioned. How he was loved! One of his cyclists is wounded, the skull cleft open, the hole being big enough to put one's fist in. Instead of being at once discharged, he wishes first to return to his officer. " My Captain, did you really think that I would ever have gone off without saying good-bye! " " Wounded as he was, having already obtained his discharge, he twice, both in coming and going back, had to pass through the fire of a barrage, and what a barrage! " writes Clement Tonnerre himself, " simply out of gratitude for a little kindness I had shown him."

Of the same strength of faith and Christian valour was Joseph Ollé-Laprune, the son of the philosopher. He exchanged the Staff Office for the fighting-line, well aware of the dangers ahead. " I have made my sacrifice to God without restriction." Each morning he renewed this sacrifice, particularly if he was able to hear Mass and to communicate. " Offering himself," says his biographer, " as a victim in union with the perfect Victim, having obtained the renewal of the same sublime offering of the lives depending on his life (his wife and his mother)."

We are too near the war to reveal all the ascensions of soul of which it was the occasion. When the time comes to search out the records of that heroic epoch it will be a cause of wonder and admiration to see to what a high degree the splendour of Catholicism radiated throughout the whole army.

. . . .

Sacrifice is already magnificent when from a spirit

of Christian duty—as was the case with a multitude —a man gives his life for his country. How much sublimer still when, out of fidelity to his faith, he consents or offers himself to die as a martyr.

Père de Foucauld knew that probably not a single Tuareg would be converted within a hundred years, but that as a result of his life buried away in the desert sands and, as he dared to hope, from the shedding of his blood, harvests would one day spring up in the heart of the Sahara.

Who does not know of that strange and impressive hall of the Martyrs at the Seminary of Foreign Missions in the Rue de Bac, at Paris, where have been gathered together the venerated remains of some of those who, in modern times, gave their lives for Christ: the Blessed Perboyre and Clet, Lazarists; the Ven. Peter Dumoulin Borie, Ven. Augustus Chapdelaine, Ven. Charles Cornay, Ven. Francis Jaccard, and yet others; Père Chicard, who, when young, hesitated between these three careers, "monk, bandit or cavalier," or the incomparable Théophane Venard, beheaded, when thirty-one years old, at Tonkin, on February 2nd, 1861. His letters sent to his parents from his iron cage before his martyrdom are marvels of poetic fervour, burning zeal, filial and fraternal love, and the total gift of self to God.

Twenty-five years previously, Jean Charles Cornay, of the Foreign Missions of Paris, had thus written with heroic simplicity from his cage, a short time before his martyrdom:

" FROM MY CAGE,
" *August 18th*, 1837.

" MY DEAR FATHER AND MOTHER,—My blood has

already flowed during my torments and is yet to flow two or three more times before I have my arms and legs and head cut off. The thought of the pain you will feel on learning these details has already made me shed many tears, but also, the thought that I shall be near God to intercede for you when you read this letter has consoled me, both for myself and for you. Do not lament the day of my death, since it will put an end to my sufferings and will be the beginning of my happiness. My torments themselves are not as cruel as they might be; no further torture will be inflicted upon me till I am healed of my present wounds. I shall not be pinched with the tweezers nor dragged about like M. Marchand, and, supposing that they cut off my four limbs, four men will do it at the same time, and a fifth will cut off my head; thus I shall not have much to suffer. Console yourselves then; in a little while all will be over and I shall be awaiting you in heaven.

"J. C. CORNAY."

On June 21st, 1870, in the Chinese city of Tien-Tsin, the Sisters of Charity who had gone out there to tend the sick and teach the children, were massacred, at the same time as two Lazarists, a Frenchman, Claude Chevrier, and a Chinese, Father Ou. Six of these Sisters were French, two Belgian, one Italian and one Irish. The Italian, Sister Andréoni, had predicted that she would be hacked to death: others would share in her happiness. The thought of martyrdom hardly ever left the Community. "They talked of it at recreation," relates Henri Bordeaux, "like schoolgirls looking out from the garden to see if love is not coming."

It was a subject delightful and unknown. On ironing days, when a cornette displayed a dazzling whiteness, one of the Sisters suggested: " How would it be to set this aside for the great day! " All met their deaths by strangling, together with a Chinese virgin, who, having refused to give up the altar vessels, was run through with a sabre.

What deeds of heroism are to be gleaned from the accounts of the rising of the Boxers about 1900![1] Heroism of missionaries. the Fathers Andlauer, Isoré, Denn and Mangin,[2] for example; heroism of adult Christians, both men and women; heroism, yet more marvellous, of children. A young Christian household had to take to flight; the little girl could scarcely lisp; her mother taught her three words: *Tien tchou kiao*, " Catholic religion." She feared, admirable Christian as she was, lest after their torments the child would be spared and become a pagan, and she had thus taught her how to reply to the Boxers. The father was killed, then the mother; the little one was so tiny that the executioners were seized with pity.

" Thou art not a Christian, thou at least."

She had a moment's hesitation; she tried to recall the lesson which fright had sent rather astray, and all at once cried out: " Religion, religion." The

---

[1] The Sacred Congregation of Rites published, in 1927, a decree whereby the Holy Father approved the introduction of the cause of Beatification of the 2,418 Christians put to death at that time.

[2] In March, 1927, the papers announced the murder by the Canton soldiery, of the two Jesuits, P. Dugout and P. Varana, at Nankin. A third, P. Jacquinot, was only saved by a miracle. In January, a Spanish Dominican had been cowardly assassinated at Foo-Chow.

other words would not come. But as soon as they began to caress her, her eyes grew terrible and she cried out again: "Religion, religion."

"She has drunk the magic potion of the Christians," exclaimed one of the Boxers; and raising his great sword, he cleft her in twain.

Here is another, rather older. The Boxers had killed the mother and five children. Barbara, twelve and a half years old, succeeds in escaping. Before harbouring her, one of her relations tells her: "If thou dost not apostatize, it is useless to enter." She leaves the village, and falls in with the Boxers.

"Art thou a Christian?"

"Yes."

"Thy kinsfolk?"

"All killed."

"Wilt thou apostatize?"

"No."

"We are going to set the knife to work."

They hang her on a tree, and hold the knife near her ear: "Is it yes?"

"No."

The knife slowly enters. An old man intervenes. She is reprieved, but left on the gibbet. The old man sets her free. On entering a village a woman, moved by the sight of the blood which is still flowing, receives her, and hides her for five months in a hole covered with branches. That is something to bear in mind.[1]

To Pierre Niou Tai-t'siel-i, a little Corean, thirteen years old, his father, on being led away to prison, had left this last counsel: "Pierre, the

[1] Under the title *Histoires Chinoises*, P. Lebbe has published some beautiful episodes of Christian bravery in the Celestial Empire.

great ones of this earth, however powerful they be, cannot gather the stars, but he who remains faithful to the Sovereign Master will see Heaven."

The little boy, on being recognized as a Christian, was condemned to be tortured. While the blows dealt by a cudgel rained down upon him, Pierre smiled. A soldier thrust a lance into his flesh.

" Wilt thou remain Christian? "

"Yes."

" Well, then, swallow this raspberry! " And he was given a burning coal.

Of his own will Pierre opened his mouth. Fourteen times the torture was repeated. Fourteen times the child remained steadfast. They had to strangle him in prison.

Pierre Niou was beatified by Pius XI on July 5th, 1925, as well as Mgr. Imbert, bishop of Corea, himself likewise a martyr.

From China let us pass on to Africa. Scarcely any older than Pierre Niou, those glorious pages of Mivanga, king of Uganda, accused of " praying," that is to say of being Christians, chose rather than deny the faith to be pierced by a lance, to have their heads cut off, and to be burnt alive, to the number of twenty-six. Three, accounted too young, were spared.

" Where is my faggot, the one for me? " each cried, wishing to accompany their brothers in the faith to the last.

Even the executioner's son was massacred, but out of pity for his father, he was not burnt alive, but first killed by a blow at the back of his neck.

Is this all? No. The peoples of America have also their martyrs. This is what a Mexican priest writes in November, 1926: " We are living at a time of truly horrible tyranny; the continual persecution is at its apogee and has reached a degree such as we could never have imagined. It is enough to be known as a Catholic to lose all security, and even, if possible, the right to live. Every day we learn that the police have made their descent upon some house where Mass was being celebrated, and taken the priest prisoner (sometimes clad in his vestments) and all those who were assisting at the Mass."

This goes as far as the shedding of blood. On January 3rd, 1927, Valencia Gallardo, Sauveur Vargas, Ezéchiel Gomez and Nicholas Navarro, belonging to the Mexican Society of Catholic Youth of Léon, were arrested and cruelly put to death. When his wife, overcome with tears, showed him his young baby, the first of these replied:

" Had I ten children, I would leave them all for God."

At the place of execution, as he was encouraging his companions, the impatient executioner cut out his tongue.

The second died crying out, " For God and for His glory."

His mother, seventy years of age, exclaimed:

" They have not chosen to give me back the body of my son, but his body does not matter; this morning I confided his soul to the Heart of Jesus."

The third said to his mother:

" I want to die, for I know that our Lord will accept my blood for the salvation of our country."

From the last, Nicholas Navarro, these words rang out at the place of execution, words which recall those of the great Garcia Moreno:

" I die, but it is for Jesus Christ Who dieth not."

The newspaper agencies keep careful silence on these facts.[1] The facts are there. Whoever wishes may verify them. Again: Don Mateo Correa, aged sixty-two, was parish priest at Vapraraiso (Zacatecas). Driven out of his parish by the persecution, he lived in a hacienda in San José de Llanetes, the property of Don José Muranda. On January 30th, 1927, he was asked to go to a dying man. He set out with the Blessed Sacrament, accompanied by Don José, but on the way met the troops of Eulogio Otriz. The two men were arrested and separated. On February 9th, a mutilated corpse, that of Mateo Correa, was found in the neighbourhood of Durango. The good priest had been assassinated. Since then, amongst other odious murders, one which calls for special attention is that of the young Jesuit, P. Pro, whose touching martyrdom was recorded by P. Dudon in *Etudes*.[2]

Like many Frenchwomen in the Great Revolution,

---

[1] Most of the daily papers published without a word of protestation, without a sign of revulsion, the following information communicated to them by a Roman agency :

" THE RELIGIOUS WAR IN MEXICO.

" Rome.—The Secretariat of the Commission of Mexican bishops announces that it has received the following news of the atrocities of the religious war in Mexico. At Toluca, a young Catholic woman was crucified and afterwards shot as she hung on her cross. At Guadalajara, a priest was sprinkled with petrol and then burnt alive. In the city of Mexico, seventeen priests were led from a fortress to the cemetery of Dolorès and shot on the edge of a pit dug in advance. Several of these were buried alive. The spectacle was so horrible that one of the grave-diggers went mad."

[2] March 5th, 1928. Charming notice by P. Couvreur, published at the *Apostolate of Prayer* at Toulouse.

the young Mexican women, by their courage and spirit, likewise bear witness to the heroism of their faith. The following episode of a young girl of eighteen is told: The troops had received the order to fire on a group of Catholics defending their Church; this intrepid Christian girl placed herself resolutely in front of the soldiers, exclaiming: " Before killing the others, kill me."

Poor country! But what a glorious religion which gives such courage to its martyrs!

.   .   .   .

Touching as these traits may be, they are less impressive from the point of view with which we are now concerned than the following reflexion; namely, that it is the high *doctrinal* standard of Catholic holiness of our day which gives it unparalleled value.

By this we mean that at every period there may be and has been Christian bravery, holiness, Catholicism practised in its fullness. What most strikes the competent observer is that holiness in our times is manifested as a spontaneous logical flowering of a Catholicism never better understood; it is that the doctrinal elements animating this great Christian effort towards the perfection of Christianity are of the highest value; it is that holiness of the present day is of great depth, and more closely linked perhaps than in the past with what is loftiest and most important in our Catholic dogma. We need only point out two characteristics: the indwelling of the Blessed Trinity in our souls through sanctifying grace, and our obligation of sharing in the Redemption of the world by Christ as being His members.

A lightning survey in these two directions.

As P. Foch observed in a letter relating to Elisabeth of the Trinity of the Carmel at Dijon, one of the essential points of Catholic dogma is the doctrine of the Divine indwelling in the soul through Baptism. It seems as if the Holy Spirit is directing a great number towards a deeper comprehension of this treasure. The great evil of our day is laicism. God places the remedy side by side with the evil. He urges Catholic souls to enter more deeply into the supernatural; He engrafts Catholic holiness upon a more certain comprehension of the " donum Dei."

Elisabeth of the Trinity is too well known for us to need to insist upon her. Let us pass on to the writings of Marie Saint Anselm of the White Sisters of Our Lady of Africa. On February 25th, 1917, she writes with her blood, in her journal: " He is drawing me more and more to live an interior life, to keep silence, to be content with Him." On April 24th: " Yes, I must be cloistered, but the cloistered White Sister. My own cloister is my Trinity. Jesus brings the whole Trinity with Him. For the first time I thus feel the presence of the Father and the active love of the Three towards One Another, within me."

The young Benedictine, Pie de Hemptinne, speaks in the same way, as does also Sophie de Claye, a nun of Marie Réparatrice.

" The soul is the abode where we must dwell," the fervent disciple of Dom Marmion wrote in his notes, and the holy life of this young religious renders beautiful homage to the formation which the justly appreciated author of *Christ the Life of the Soul* and *Christ in His Mysteries* gave to him as his novice master. " Our Lord alone has the right to enter into this abode. On this account it is worthy of the name of Sanctuary. It is the solitude where man meets with his God and learns to know and love Him. . . . There are some who give access to the spirit of darkness by giving themselves up to sin; they drive away the Spirit of God and prefer hatred to love. There are others who dread opening their hearts to God, because they are daunted by the austerity of chaste love and know not the charm of the Divine solitude of the soul. These are children of the world, who are blinded by their levity and separated from the One True God by their tepidity. There are yet others who have opened their souls entirely to God and ever possess Him that they may live there with Him, and know and love Him. These alone understand that the soul is the abode where we must dwell."

In the writings of Sophie de Claye—writings prefaced by Father de la Brière—are some exceptionally beautiful pages for the Feast of Pentecost, on the Holy Spirit, the "sweet Guest of the soul." Neither is it irrelevant to know that in June, 1877, Sister Mary of Jesus Crucified, a Lay Sister of the Carmel of Bethlehem, who died in the odour of sanctity in the following year, gave Mgr. Bracco a petition for the Pope, in which she said to the Sovereign Pontiff on our Lord's behalf: "The world and religious communities seek for novelties in the way of devotions and neglect true devotion to the Paraclete. Even in the seminaries it is neglected."

But if we are "deified," it is due to Christ. In order to restore to us the supernatural gifts lost by original sin, the Word was made Man, but He incorporated us in Himself. Saint Paul, who, with Saint John, is the great theologian of this doctrine, seems to be better known than hitherto, and a certain number of souls dream of attaining the Christian ideal which he sets before them. Hence the particularly virile character of their striving towards holiness.

Catherine O'Neil, the first mistress of novices at the *Assumption*, whose valuable notes, it is to be hoped, will not be left indefinitely in obscurity, had unquestionably a special gift for. practising and teaching this solid doctrine. Her great‧devotion was devotion to Christ as Head of the Mystical Body. " What I have to do," she said, " is to reproduce within myself the life of Christ, and devote myself to His mysteries." Our Lord asked this of her, " desiring that her whole being should be entirely given up to His designs. Be Emmanuel! (Catherine O'Neil's name in religion was Mother Teresa Emmanuel.) It is not my will that you should any longer live your own life, but that it should be I Who live in you." And, in her humility, she adds : " It is a kind of interior struggle between Jesus Who appropriates my being that He may use it according to His ends as if it were His own, and I who want to keep the ownership of this being." " I felt," she says again, " utterly condemned to lose my life, my whole life, not by men, but by God." We recognize the *Jam non ego, Christus*, of Saint Paul.

In Marie-Aimée de Jésus, of the Carmel in the Avenue de Saxe, is to be found the same note, even more accentuated if possible. She makes a vow of doing always what is most pleasing to God so as to atone for the defection of Renan, and she feels impelled to write a life of our Lord to counteract the too famous *Vie de Jésus*. This was her plan of sanctification: to disappear, so that Christ alone, within her, should live and radiate; to become a living semblance of Jesus Christ.

As an integral part of Christ Jesus, we have not only to become as far as possible other Christs; we have to extend His action. He has identified us with His own Person: *I am the Vine, you are the branches*, solely to unite us to His work. Through our baptismal vocation, we are the redeemers of the world, because of our oneness with Christ, the Redeemer of the world. People are learning to understand this better; hence this strong attraction towards reparation. We have spoken elsewhere on this characteristic of holiness in the Church at the present time and may here content ourselves with a brief mention.

Where would it be possible to find a keener perception of our share in the redemption than in the following: Marie Deluil-Martiny, the foundress of the *Filles Cœur de Jésus*, one of the women who have best written on our duty of filling up the sufferings of Christ; she was assassinated by an anarchist on February 27th, 1884; P. Lyonnard, the holy author of the *Apostolat de la Souffrance*, or, in Belgium, P. Lintelo. Among the laity: General Sonis; the generous Louis Peyrot, founder of the *Union Catholique des Malades*; Marie Brotel, favoured with wonderful revelations on the priesthood and the holiness requisite for the priest, on the necessity of the *cor unum* between all religious orders and the members of the ecclesiastical hierarchy, and on love for the Church and the Pope; Thérèse Durnerin, foundress of the *Amis des Pauvres*, or again Marie-Antoinette de Geuser, niece of the learned and holy Father Léonce de Grandmaison. It was her ideal to reproduce so faithfully the fullness of life " in Christ " that she might in the most perfect degree content the Master's longing: *Ut sint consummati in unum* " Consummata." [1]

This need of intimate union, and these aspirations towards partaking in the world's redemption, most frequently result from contact with the Host. In proof of this need we may recall Mlle. Tamisier, the initiator, together with Philibert Vrau, of International Eucharistic Congresses; or again Eustelle Harpain, who died at the age of twenty-nine after being sacristan of a Church in Vendée for seven years. P. Eymard said of her: " I am convinced that the virgin of Saint-Pallas was the precursor of that triumph of the Eucharist which we now witness."

Fifteen years after her death, three young girls of Toulouse grouped themselves together and addressed a petition to Marie Eustelle asking her to be their honorary president. This was the germ of the little *Société de Jésus-Hostie*, which ten years later was to develop into that of the *Servantes de Jésus dans le Très Saint Sacrement*. Mlle. Guibert, the survivor of these three, was given the name of Mother Marie Eustelle, after her. On January 12th, 1921, Marie-Eustelle's cause was introduced.

Mother Thérèse de la Croix, foundress of the *Gardienne Adoratrices de Saint-Sacrement*, who was to meet her death in the bombardment of Comines on November 18th, 1916, was likewise called to spread devotion to the Eucharist; her family were not very fervent Christians. The Eucharist, first received by her when she was twelve years old, was the leaven which gave her, in spite of her early

[1] Her life has been published by l'A. de la P., Toulouse.

repugnances, the desire for the religious and Eucharistic life. At the beginning she aspired to Carmel;
then Mgr. Dupanloup admitted her to Saint Aignan,
of which she became the second foundress, and
where she introduced special devotion to Jesus in
the Blessed Sacrament.[1]

The centre of the Catholic religion is Jesus Christ,
the Incarnate Word, Jesus prolonging His sojourn
amongst us under the appearances of the Host. But
the centre of this centre is love. The inmost soul
of this effort, carried even to folly by Christ in order
to restore Divine life to us, is the folly of His love
for us. The heart of the world is Jesus Christ, and
the Heart of Christ is the Sacred Heart. Never has
devotion to the Sacred Heart been better understood
than in our own time, and that is again one of the
reasons why Catholic holiness of the present day is
so abundant and so intense. How many give themselves to this Heart? How many Institutes are
founded in Its name and honour or make profession
of working only for Its glory? Was not this one
of the promises of the Sacred Heart to Saint
Margaret Mary: " I will make fervent souls holy "?
He keeps His promise.

Here again names must be given. We cannot
pass over these, out of many others: Mother Mary
of the Divine Heart, born de Droste-Vischering,
raised up by God to ask Leo XIII to consecrate the
human race to the Heart of Jesus. Louise Thérèse
de Montaignac, leaving to her daughters, at the
same time as the care of beautiful works of zeal,
notably the " Samuels," the spiritual flame whereby
they live: " O Jesus! eternal Life in the Person of
the Father, Life of souls made in Your Image, make

[1] Her *Life* is published by de Gigord, Paris.

known, reveal Your Heart!''—a cry never henceforth to be forgotten. Marie Adèle Garnier[1] (1838-1924), who founded an Institute of Adoration at Montmartre; one of the Communities she formed is installed on the site where Tyburn gallows once stood, and where her daughters now pray, meditate and expiate, particularly for the return of England to Catholic unity. Louise Marguerite de la Touche, who died at the age of forty-seven, on May 14th, 1915, foundress of *Béthanie du Sacré Cœur* and of the *Alliance Sacredotale Universelle des Amis du Sacré Cœur*. Her autobiography, written in obedience to her director, P. Alfred Charrier, has been published. When eleven years of age, she made a vow of virginity; when twenty-three a life of Saint Aloysius gave a fresh impetus to her life; she was admitted to the Visitation at Romans on November 20th, 1890, entered into the mystic way, notably from June, 1902, and consummated her last years in a life of devotedness and immolation for the priesthood.

. . . .

It is indeed a cause of regret to be obliged to omit so many representative figures, but so it must be! Let us at least point out the power of Catholic holiness as evinced by the wonderful movement in the way of *conversions* during these latter years, and among numerous *vocations*, some of more than ordinary significance.

Numerous conversions of Anglicans and members of the Orthodox church; conversions of unbelievers, and this, most generally, not in uncultured circles, and in virtue of a more or less herdlike faith, but

[1] In religion Mère Marie de St. Pierre du Sacré Cœur [Trans.]

on the part of intellectual, reflective personalities, not arriving at a decision until after deep study of the problems involved: Ruville, Benson, Claudel, Psichari, Rivière, and hundreds of others.

Vocations likewise and to a still greater extent evince the thirst after holiness which Catholic notions and life stimulate.

From their adjoining bedrooms, a little boy and girl, brother and sister, nine and seven years old, carry on a dialogue together.

" Jeanne! "

" What? "

" Didn't you know? There is a good God."

" What does that mean? "

They chatter on, and every evening begin over again. The small boy repeats what has been told him at school. One day the parents, unbelievers, happen to overhear. They are impressed. Grace begins to work. George and Jeanne Doussol are baptized at the same time as their parents. The brother enters the Dominican Order, the sister that of the Carmelites.

A few years after the war, Count Claude d'Elbée and the Countess his wife decide to give themselves to God. He, a brilliant officer of the French Staff, enters at Picpus; she becomes Sister Claire du Cœur de Jésus at the Carmel of Louvain.

Likewise ordained priest by Cardinal Mercier, Lieutenant-General Count Francois de Grunne, in religion Dom Dominique of the Order of Saint Benedict; it was Whit Sunday, 1923: foremost among those present were his sons and his son-in-law, Counts Charles, Eugène, Willy and Xavier de Grunne and Count André de Montalembert.

Here an officer of genius exchanges his spurs for

the coarse serge of Saint John of God. He is one day pursued by a band of young ruffians, who cry out at the top of their voices: " Down with the Jesuits! "

" I am not a Jesuit," calmly replies Brother Magalon as he turns and faces them. " I am a brother of Saint John of God, and I look after the insane. At your service, gentlemen! "

Lawyers, sailors. With the intention of following in the steps of Father de Foucauld, a barrister of Nancy and a Vice-Admiral join the ranks of the priesthood. Both ordained by the bishop of Carthage, they pitch their tents on the edge of the Sahara, counting upon the prayers of the apostle of the Hoggar to fructify their apostolate. Vice-Admiral Malcor had had a brilliant career; he had commanded the post of Bizerte. He prefers his gandourah to his stars.

Under the title " *Du Gouvernement au Cloître*," it was recently announced that a Chinese Prime Minister, M. René Lou-Tseng-Tsiang, had entered the Benedictine Abbey of Saint André in Bruges.

Here are some examples among women: An Italian actress, the star of the Comic Opera, Rosina Storchia, " la Storchia," as they say in the theatrical world, does not find in her art enough to fill her life; she gives up the stage and enters the Convent of Saint Clare at Assisi. Eve Lavallière,[1] on her part, sacrifices human glory to consecrate herself to a life of entire obscurity, prayer and renunciation; again, under the name of Sister Paul Dominique, Mme. Paul Adam, wife of the vigorous author of *Trust* and of *La Force*, seeks at the

[1] Her death on July 10th, 1929, was recently announced. [Trans.]

Convent of Pensier, near Fribourg in Switzerland, the fullness of peace which the world cannot give.

An ardent passion for holiness is found in all these souls! How mighty then is Christ, how Divine His religion, which calls for such sacrifices, and inspires such intensity of love, such moral elevation of soul.

Amidst the perplexities of the hour, this enables us to look the future in the face. More than aught else besides in the century in which we live saints are needed. It is almost fifty years ago since Mgr. Baunard, at the beginning of his biography of Madeleine Sophie Barat, dared to recall this in emphatic terms,[1] and during these last months, in *La Primauté du Spirituel*, Maritain brings out clearly the present necessity, we might even say the urgent need, of holiness: " Still more necessary

---

[1] " When a guilty society is threatened perhaps with a new deluge of fire, it is not quite irrelevant to count the just ones in its bosom, for we know that ten such weigh more than a thousand others in the balance of God. Someone has said ' that saints consecrate the world.' I add that they preserve it. They are the true, the only *conservatives* of a world that turns them into ridicule, and in fact owes them its preservation. The worth of a country depends in His estimation on the number of saints it has produced. This is so much the case that the day on which the earth no longer sent saints to heaven would be the one marked for its destruction. . . . They march onward whilst others wander; they *edify* in the true sense of the word whilst others pull down; they are here below the instruments of life; others are, more or less, instruments of death. Love, prayer, example, and sacrifice, of which they are the perpetual exemplification, are continually offering a contrast to our crimes. They protest against them on earth and they make up for them in the sight of heaven." Author's Introduction, pp. xvii-xviii. (Translated by Lady Georgiana Fullerton.)

than combined action—and moreover constituting a higher condition—is (holiness). . . . That is what the anguish of the present day requires before all else. The world demands saints." On a previous page he says: "Christian heroism will one day become the one and only solution of the problems of life. Then, as God proportions His grace to our needs, and tempts none beyond their strength, an abundant harvest of holiness will doubtless be seen to coincide with the worst state of human history."

How fully this prognostic appears to be approaching realization! The near past is for us a sure guarantee of the future.

CONCLUSION

PERHAPS this all too rapid sketch may give some idea of the power of sanctification Christ's Church possesses in this twentieth century, as in every other century, and certainly no less than in any other. The principles are sure and efficacious; the results conclusive.

It may be said: This is very true, and unless prepared to be accused of sectarianism or lack of discernment, none can deny how glorious is the panorama of Catholic holiness ranging from the most glowing colours to almost imperceptible tints. But are you not forgetting the other side of the question? If the Church possesses such an effectual power of sanctification, how is it that there are so many Christians who are far from being saints?

. . . .

To begin with a response *ad hominem*. To the charge that there is not enough holiness among the children of the Catholic Church, we ask in our turn: Is there more elsewhere? Compared with any other religion whatsoever, does she not bear the palm? What religion do you know that sanctifies its members to the same extent? If you are yourself a child of the Church, how do you gainsay this reproach? If you are indifferent, where are your virtues, that they may be judged by comparison? As for the Church's enemies, are they in a position to compare their virtues and those of Catholics? Someone has dared to say—the words sound brutal, but are they far from the truth?—" Very often it would be sufficient vindication for the Church to bring the lives of her detractors to the light of day."

But we confess that there is a falling short. Such statements as these are loudly proclaimed. " Supposing that all who are Christians in name were Christians in fact, there would no longer be any social questions," declared Clemenceau. He is right, but let it be well understood that the lack of holiness in certain Catholics is not because they obey their principles, but because they are unfaithful to them. It is on human weakness that the blame must be laid, and not on the powerlessness of the Catholic doctrine to sanctify.

Yet more brutal than Clemenceau, this is what Nietzsche says: " If your faith makes you happy, give yourselves out as such! Your countenances have always done more harm to your faith than your arguments have done. If the glad tidings of your Bible were written on your face you would have no need to be so zealous in exacting belief in the authority of this Book; your words and deeds would continually render the Bible superfluous, a new Bible would ever have its source within you."

As we have seen, this new Bible, this apologetic having its source in the virtues, exists, and we must not let a few trees hinder us from seeing the forest. What is proved by the cockle growing among the wheat? That the Church upon earth is as yet only militant. She possesses all that is necessary to make her members perfect; she does not claim that all her members are so. "The Church is not a society of the perfect," an English author very justly observes, "but a school for the imperfect. To confound the Church militant with the Church triumphant is an already ancient error."

May we hazard this further response? If the Catholic Church which possesses so great a power of sanctification has not yet sanctified all around her; if all those in her own bosom do not live in the perfection of Christianity, what conclusion are we to draw? That the Church is a failure? No. It is simply that not only must the passions and vices of each one be taken into account, but also the duration of time. Who knows whether the world is not yet young! We are perhaps only witnessing the first feeble flights of the human race. Do not the greater number of civilized people appear as little better than undeveloped primitives, as far as the soul is concerned? The Gospel has scarcely made any way as yet. All has yet to be done, or nearly all. La Bruyère wrote: "Everything has been said and we come too late." Certainly not that. Or if much has been said, nothing has yet been done. Among the nations. among different classes, among individuals, in the depth of each soul, in ourselves who read these lines, how far has the Gospel reached, what is the extent of its action? One ounce of the true Gospel, wherever found, is sufficient to make all new. But such care is taken to act in all things irrespective of the Gospel. The world is young. Christ has not yet given His full measure. Vast barbarism still reigns, and it truly appears as if we were only at the dawn of things. The veil is being slowly raised, the grain of mustard seed has scarcely sprouted above the ground, the leaven has only been cast in a few places, and where it has been cast, antagonistic influences have destroyed or diminished its power. But of what great things is not the Gospel capable wherever it may freely penetrate and shed forth its light?

Who can tell what Christ's Kingdom upon earth will be a thousand years hence? Not only will the Church grow in extent, but it will grow in perfection. Magnificent saints are yet to appear; magnificent saints, at this present hour, are being born and prepared; and who knows whether, at the very moment in which we end these lines, a child, whom the Church will one day canonize—as she has already canonized so many of her sons and daughters—is not already lying in some near or distant cradle!

Beautiful and numerous as are the saints—those of bygone days and those of the present—fruitful as the sanctifying action of the Church has ever been throughout the world, we do not think that our Lord came only to bring about these humble results. Doubtless holiness *de jure*, like Catholicism *de jure*, is, strictly speaking, alone necessary, and these are independent of time. The world may end to-morrow; duration adds nothing to them.[1]

But it is not the same with holiness *de facto*. How many of the human race yet remain to be sanctified! A thousand million of Pagans; and among those who know Christ, deduction made of heretics and schismatics in good faith, who act according to their lights, deduction too made of the faithful who are truly faithful—those saints we

---

[1] Except a most eloquent confirmation, evidently.

have mentioned of whatever degree—how many would remain who enter deeply into the spirit of the Gospel.

It is to co-operate in this work of sanctification that every man has been created. God grant that these rapid glances may help some souls to rise higher, and make of them, for the edification of those who are to people the future ages, more faithful reproductions of the Saint above all others, the One only perfect Saint, our Lord Jesus Christ.